THE REDEMPTION OF DEMOCRACY

THE
REDEMPTION
OF DEMOCRACY

The Coming Atlantic Empire

By

HERMANN RAUSCHNING

ALLIANCE BOOK CORPORATION
NEW YORK

Translated from the German by Barrows Mussey

COPYRIGHT 1941 BY

ALLIANCE BOOK CORPORATION

Forthcoming British title:

THE BEAST FROM THE ABYSS

*Who is like unto the beast? who
is able to make war with him?*
—REVELATIONS

PRINTED IN THE UNITED STATES OF AMERICA

AMERICAN BOOK—STRATFORD PRESS, INC., NEW YORK

Contents

PART ONE

1. The Steerage of the New Mayflower   3
2. The Shattering of Security   9
3. The Revolution of Nihilism Is Universal 23
4. The Very Heart of This War 33
5. The Seafaring Democracies 41

PART TWO

1. Hitler's Technique Again 63
2. The New Social Basis 83
3. The Unseen Revolution 107
4. The Assimilation of the Revolution 129
5. Leviathan 163
6. The Redemption of Democracy 177
7. The Mystery of Iniquity 195
8. The "Finest Hour" 229

Part I

The Steerage of the New Mayflower

WE ARE UNDER WAY. Foaming, the times race with us. Or do we only imagine we are moving? Is it merely the stormy tide of our times rushing headlong beneath our keel? Whither are we bound in the steerage of this our vessel, on the hard planks, in foul air, with no stars, the deep below, the snarl of danger above us? We are lying in the underground shelters of our city and land as if in the steerage of a new *Mayflower*. Torn from security and comfort, we are sailing away from home and all we know into stern, remote, uncharted seas. All London, this whole land of England, is the vessel. We are bound for the future, for the land of new days. Hope is with us; confidence makes the dark voyage bearable.

Hope we have. Dream pictures accompany us. We dream, we brood, we see the tremulous outline of things to come. We see them monstrously enlarged; perhaps we hope for the miraculous. Perhaps we believe we can escape from monotony and toil for good and all. Perhaps we see only the peril, the suffering, and the blackness behind and about us — and not the toil and trouble ahead.

What are we leaving behind us? What are we seeking ahead? These are the questions of our transitional age, an age between battles and in the midst of battles, an age of voyages and discoveries, when the current of an inscrutable fate sweeps us loose from all familiar things.

* * *

I have put out the light, and I am looking through my window, which opens above a tennis court. Thick masses of smoke from a fire down among the docks move across the sky, making a ruddy twilight. Searchlights flash across the heavens; their shafts sweep together into bundles, part again, and vanish. It is a real night of the Apocalypse. The bombers move in roaring circles above us. Bursts — distant — closer; the whistle of bombs very near, and the quiver of heavy hits hard by. I go down to find fellow humans. It is the old urge to be together in danger and distress. Now that the barking of the anti-aircraft guns, deep and shrill, is mingling with the groans of exploding bombs, sleep upstairs can no longer be thought of. Incendiary bombs have fallen on our roof, and high explosive on our tennis court.

We have made ourselves at home in the cellar below. I have set up a table in the telephone booth. There I can work without disturbing the others. We have adjusted ourselves to each other. We lie on blankets and mattresses, overcoats and cushions.

There is the elderly married couple. They sleep quietly, one feeling safe near the other, with an affection that bears witness to long custom. Here is the middle-aged couple. Their exterior harmony seems only a good front put on a bad business. One

4

man is reading, blanketed with his greatcoat, with a suitcase for a pillow. There is the old spinster. She seems to have thought out a special method, a patent device to avoid being hit. Cushions and blankets are piled high on the floor; the air is almost intolerable.

From where I am writing I can just see the tiny feet of the young woman moving playfully. A young couple, he in khaki, perhaps just married, perhaps courting; both are youthful, happy, carefree. The young woman is constantly giggling and chattering, despite bomb bursts and minor earthquakes.

A golden-haired, plump-cheeked one-year-old is a new member of our sleeping-club. Trusting, and not in the least shy of all the strangers, the tiny fellow keeps crawling from mother to father. They are guests at the hotel next door, which has had to be vacated because of a time bomb. He takes his bottle placidly, and goes to sleep. Gradually our hotel basement is jammed full. Yonder are the Free French captains, with a knack of making themselves at home under difficult conditions that bespeaks practice.

The earth rocks as if in an earthquake. One of the women, scared, sobs loudly. It was a large bomb bursting near by. The Frenchmen comfort her: *"C'est fini."* Then abrupt silence. The beast has withdrawn into the darkness.

People are living like this everywhere in the cellars of the vast city. They are living like this in the other towns, large and small. They are forming new communities, flung together from many countries and levels of society. Barriers fall, prejudices evaporate. We are in the melting pot; we are being fused for the new molds

5

— masters and servants, laborers and employers all in the same extremity.

There are thousands of Anderson shelters, tiny lifeboats in an open sea. They give no elbow-room. You hear the roar of the bombers and the barking of the guns. The little crew of such a boat is utterly alone in the midst of the endless universe — alone face to face with destiny, with an inscrutable force, a cosmic power in human employ. Is it mere chance, or does fate decide who shall be hit? A new fear comes alive, the old, ageless fear for life, born of the primeval ages when man was delivered from the womb of the beast, when he gave names to good and evil forces, and tried to interpret life. And now we are tossed back, tens of centuries back. What is the sense of people's diverting themselves here with card-playing, there with whiskey, singing together yonder, or talking of work and the future? Everything has grown unimportant. Man is faced once again with the black of night, the inconceivable power of unreadable destiny; he is shaken loose from all the securities of a domesticated life.

And then there are the great subterranean chambers, the huge basements. All kinds of people gather there. In them there is no community. People remain aloof, form cliques, assure themselves of regular places. Praying and brooding people who want quiet gather in one spot. The card-players and the wags meet elsewhere. Families, with their common cares, stick together. Neighborhoods, streets, have rendezvous.

Then there are the Underground stations. Thousands crouch or lie on stairs and along the walls, with pillows and blankets, food and knitting. Here are the settled denizens, yonder the rovers. The settled people jealously guard their regular places, and defend them against interlopers; the others, modern nomads, roam from cellar to cellar. They are in search of an ideal — the absolutely safe refuge.

And above us this old city is crashing into ruins bit by bit. It is slow work. Such destruction is not easily completed. But every night the dead zone in the great stone creature grows. None knows how it will end, how it can end. Yet one thing everyone feels: as the old continent once sank away beyond the horizon from the Pilgrim Fathers on the old *Mayflower,* so now this age and the present are fading before us. The whole world of yesterday, of today, this world of habit, is disappearing. We shall see it no more. It is a farewell forever.

2

The Shattering of Security

How DID THE DISASTER come upon us? How did it shatter the sunny days of a summer such as none remembered? War seemed remote, impossible, unreal. We were living; all the violence seemed a dream. We could breathe deep in that abundant, mellow world with its last outpouring of brilliance and gaiety; war was a horrid fairy-tale.

How could it all happen? How could that man infect a whole nation with his madness, and impose his yoke of destruction and thraldom on the world? How was it possible? This is the question on everyone's lips.

Was it not simply that no solid social or political structure remained, no inner strength? Had not the revolution come, unrecognized? Was it not even here, in this country, among the trusted men of the old Western nations — a new, evil, unheard-of revolution?

The German disintegration brought forth the revolution of nihilism. It has expanded into universal dissolution, into world revolution. The social structure has changed under the hands of those in political command. The great political order is going to pieces. New groupings are coming into being, uniting into power blocs and breaking up again. This is no mere war, with the usual aftermath. Forces that had been stored up are bursting the old dams.

What is permanent in this transformation? What is to be retained, and what cast aside? Where is the new substance? Not simply the exterior order, but the new frontiers, the new institutions?

Let us rather begin by searching for the face of this revolution that has broken out amongst us.

"Our whole European civilization, in an agony of tension that grows from decade to decade, has long been moving toward a catastrophe. What I am telling is the history of the next two centuries. I am describing what will come, what cannot now but come: 'The rise of Nihilism.' "

Nietzsche wrote those words a generation ago. National Socialism is among the political forms of this nihilism; it is not the only form, and not the final one.

What then is nihilism?

"For the supreme values to become worthless. A goal is wanting; an answer is wanting to the question *why*," Nietzsche replied. Everything was put in question; incertitude overwhelmed mankind.

There was something creeping forward, stealing its way from the edges toward the heart of our life — a many-limbed being. These bright days of summer sunlight with the smell of autumn's falling leaves — time grows confused. Already our feet rustle the dry leaves; still we do not believe the death and the devastation.

Demonic forces have burst upon our sheltered world. We experience anew the perpetual faultiness and questionableness of this brighter world that we have piled up above the real one like puffy clouds on a sultry summer day — mountains, strange figures, fabulous landscapes and ripened gold. But there is nothing real to carry your weight or lay your hand on. Our humanity is still no more than a gossamer veil over untamed and untamable forces.

More has happened here than simple mechanical conquest of an apparently invincible safety zone through the resources of a new technology. More has collapsed than just the Maginot Line. The idea of human security in general has been questioned anew.

Those incredibly lovely summer days, an almost unbroken chain of sun, warmth, and blue sky, were shattered by the new war. The new war is four-dimensional — space multiplied by time; it is irrational, outgrowing any mere linear or plane aspects of former wars. At one moment all is security, law and order, glorious peace; the next, there is an eruption of death and destruction. There are moments of war, and then we have peace again; people lounge on the chairs in Hyde Park, women go shopping, children play, and men pursue their business. Once more war is remote, implausible: it does not exist. It is but a cerebral danger, unreal to instinct and senses.

What will be the result of war in this form? Will it free us from the limited concepts of a hundred and fifty years' bourgeois security, and show us the faultiness of all outward human order? Shall we seek a basis for our tangible endeavors where it was found by former ages that could distinguish between the unchanging, and the changeable which the devout man daily prayed God to change for the better? Or shall we lose ourselves more than ever in the effort to establish an outward order that will give to everyone the greatest imaginable security against all the blows of fate? Security — not simply as a catchword for the bourgeois, the propertied citizen afraid for his property, but above all for the masses. Security, the root of all socialism; security to the point of abolishing everything that darker ages called destiny or fate. Security from disease, from passion, security from death and the hereafter, security from all supernatural forces of retribution or judgment. Security from the demons of the subconscious, of the past, of history. Security — is not this the bright light of reason?

But not alone this security of fortified lines, of fortressed zones, which might be wrenched apart or overstepped — not this alone was illusory. Illusory too is the whole concept of bourgeois security. For man himself, possessed of demons, cannot help destroying his own security again and again.

In these weeks of great trial, ought we not to get a new sense of the inadequacy of outward arrangements as human safeguards? Not that they are unnecessary or futile — quite the contrary. After the present trials we must aim more than ever toward an order in which such bursts of destructive frenzy are impossible. But is that enough? The point is rather that the illusion lies not in the safeguards, valuable as such, but in their purely external nature.

It will be replied that man has not managed to keep pace with his material inventions and institutions. But is this really pertinent? On the contrary: not merely has man been unable to keep pace spiritually with his technical progress, but his concrete institutions have caused him to wither inwardly. Yet why? Here at last is a key that might possibly open a new door to us. Is it not true after all, even in these progressive days, that man can be improved only from within — that an inner transformation is necessary before an outer one can endure?

The four-dimensional war puts in question not only 150 years of bourgeois security, but 350 years of an enlightenment that gave self-determination to man, releasing him from subservience to a higher, absolute authority. Through it the limits of a purely material order, completely emancipated from any transcendental order, are now made painfully clear. For man is man only when he centers his dispositions not upon himself and his purposes, but upon a higher end. Therefore humanism itself is the beginning of dehumanization, because it takes the self-determining man as the end and aim of existence; thus it lacks any tribunal deriving from the absolute.

What place have such theological considerations in political thinking?

Well, what becomes of a democracy when its rules are no longer inviolable — when there is no longer any common ethical basis? Are the old conventions binding in dealing with a mind that recognizes nothing but itself, its life, its right to live, its will to power? And what but belief in a transcendent order of which the human order is part can ever bring that mind to recognize anything else? The dilemma of every human order centering altogether upon man and his purposes is that it ends with total absence of freedom. It cannot assume as an element of practical will what it denies as a spiritual reality — the brotherhood of man, which exists only in God.

Enlightenment, reason, progress, the draining of the spiritual morasses in man, regulation for external security and truer justice — all these efforts at release from the pressure of existence, from the terror of life are wonderful human accomplishments. Instead of a boon they become a scourge, instead of a tool a means of oppression, if they are exalted to be the absolute human values.

PROPHETS AND PROPAGANDISTS

The Jews cast the Prophet Jeremiah into the dungeon of Malchiah, the son of Hammelech, when he prophesied the fall of Jerusalem: "This man seeketh not the welfare of this people, but the hurt," they shouted. It is an ill thing to prophesy. And how indeed could it be otherwise? If everyone foresaw the coming disaster, how could it occur? I make no complaint if certain warnings of the enormity of the coming revolution have not been seriously received. Perhaps it seemed too utterly unlikely that this strange man Hitler, risen from the dregs of the German people, and considered simply a gangster, a cork always floating to the top, should have planned down to the last detail nine years beforehand what he is now carrying out. This presupposed an accuracy of aim and far-reaching plans of a scope that people were not inclined to ascribe to this man, of all men. It was precisely Hitler's convinced adversaries who refused to believe in these terrifying enormities. They described as figments of the imagination, paid or unpaid propaganda, the things that we now know were being secretly prepared with uncanny precision.

It was not an Ebed-melech the Ethiopian who took me up like the prophet out of the mire in the dungeon where I lay that winter when my conversations with Hitler were made public; it was the brutal reality brought home by the carrying out of Hitler's plans — the attack on Scandinavia, the invasion of Holland, the disguised troops, treason and bribed government functionaries, fifth columns and the echoing overthrow of the old French democracy by the very means that this man Hitler had proclaimed on the Obersalzberg in 1932.

Will it go on like this? Will Great Britain and the Balkans, Russia and the Near East, Africa and America and the Far East have each its turn, one after another? Will this world revolution go on to the bitter end, the destruction of the old order? Or is there still a foothold? Is there a power that can oppose this revolution of nihilism? Is it the democracies?

Faith in the democracies has been rather discredited since the former leading Continental power of the democratic order proved impotent. Did not Hitler thus offer the most striking of all proof that his contempt for the old political order of controlled freedom was justified? Was not this an indication that the new reality demanded other methods of political leadership than had heretofore existed? At its innermost core had not democracy remained the system of rank that it originally was? And could such a regime endure despite the revolt of the masses, the new industrial society, the new implements of power and the new collective consciousness?

In this situation we undertake once more the task of examining the causes that made Germany National Socialist, and inquiring how National Socialism could arise at all. Did not people have inadequate conceptions of it? Where now are the days of special experts who could calculate to the dot when National Socialism was definitely bound to collapse — whether from lack of raw materials, or labor shortage, or the new inflation, and domestic indebtedness, or the inadequate supply of officers, or whatever it might be? All these economic experts, these fiscal conservatives, these experts in public opinion — they were wrong, one and all. Contrary to the nature of things, contrary to all probability, the phenomenon of National Socialism survived with ever more crushing success, subjugating its own refractory nation, overcoming the forces of stubborn resistance and resentment, eating its way through obstacles and hindrances, and feeding on opposition. What a "triumph of will-power" indeed for this man and his movement, these sweepings from dark corners!

There proved to be more involved than a simple desire for revenge and national consolidation. It was not merely the German nationalists' pressure for expansion that stood behind National Socialism. Whence did the movement get its power of contagion to infect its adversaries? How could it paralyze the will and confuse the judgments and emotions of its opponents as it did? These are questions of eminently practical importance. In the case of Germany the errors and self-deceptions that helped the rise of the nihilist revolution can be shown — mistakes made quite largely in good faith and with the best of intentions. It is possible to show beyond the particular case of Germany something widespread and generally valid — a danger that threatens everyone, our whole planet.

Why did we become National Socialists — we who were not gangsters, derelicts, people with resentments, victims of disappointment, but patriots, intelligent men of good will? I believe I am right in thinking that an answer to this question is not unnecessary even today, in the midst of the hurricane. If National Socialism were a particularly violent form of German nationalism, if the whole movement actually did serve the national aggrandizement of Germany, even though at the expense of her neighbors, then perhaps there would be some truth in the reproach laid against us not only in Germany but in England, sometimes with unconcealed scorn — the charge that we betrayed our country, whose greatness, right or wrong, was so obviously at stake. I believe the reasons that led us to turn from National Socialism in the midst of its rise to undreamed-of triumphs may help to correct current judgments of the great struggle we are now involved in.

I fear that my German émigré fellow-sufferers who did not, like me, oppose the Weimar democracy cannot be altogether acquitted of imagining things as much simpler than they really are. There is a fundamental difference in our situations, outwardly so similar. Not merely that *we* deliberately turned our backs on what we had mistakenly supported, while most of them were compelled to emigrate unwillingly as representatives of the old, overthrown order. Much greater is the difference in what we apparently have in common — the battle against the thing that has taken political shape in Germany, and our determination to regenerate democracy.

What made us oppose parliamentary democracy, the popular belief in progress, and humanistic pseudo-idealism was not irresponsibility; it was the portents and beginning of this very nihilist revolution. These signs were visible long before National Socialism, and independent of it, even in the Weimar Republic.

CONFUSIONS

Blue sky. I cannot remember that whole summer and late spring except as one single expanse of blue sky. Now the leaves are falling, prematurely yellow and dead. It smells of autumn, yet it is but early September. A lovely view across the pond in Hyde Park, the great tower of Parliament with the delicate filigree of the scaffolding in the background. We are lounging in our chairs, reading, breathing, living.

Then the sirens scream; little clouds of shrapnel burst high in the heavens; the thunder of artillery, squadrons over the city, German planes pursued by British planes. A breath-taking fight over our heads. Amazed, we still regard it as a spectacle.

Pillars of smoke go up on the horizon — fire in the City. *We* are the target. This means us. Destruction around us; death in our midst.

We are changed beings. I think we have all been transformed during these weeks and months, some of us unconsciously, some of us perhaps with grief and horror. Is not modern man, bundle of reactions that he is, simply being atomized yet further? Perhaps he is nothing now but an instrument for performing reflexes. Will the masses lose their last self-restraint, and sell their souls blindly in the end to the one who guarantees them one final grain of security?

How did it happen that this nihilism was not even perceived

outside the country that gave it its name? There is more involved than the mere typical, optimistic, liberal reaction. Perhaps something of the faith in the non-existence of evil so deeply rooted in the Anglo-Saxon outlook played a part here. That is, in the biblical sense the idols Baal and Moloch are nonentities, *elilim*. We invest them with life through our own fear or devotion. In this there is certainly a profounder wisdom than can be claimed by any Pharisaical enlightenment that puts itself beyond good and evil. But in order to be able to tell the nonentity that it is nothing and can do nothing, one must, like the Old Testament prophets, have no share in the worship of these idols. Otherwise we have the attitude of a great many Western statesmen with their roots in unfounded liberal optimism — lack of foresight, thoughtlessness, light-mindedness, and a good dash of arrogance.

But when we seek the causes of this great revolution, our ideas fall prey to a peculiar turmoil. The triumph of National Socialism is not the triumph of a wily tactician over slow-thinking victims. "As the birds that are caught in the snare; so are the sons of men snared in an evil time, when it falleth suddenly upon them." (Ecclesiastes 9, 12). We enter upon the domain of misunderstandings and temptations, which tragically distort our best efforts.

Is it true, as a radical German thinker has maintained, that in the present age there is but one direction in which anything can be successfully planned or intended, while all else is romanticism? The one direction is toward consistent mechanization, rationalization and technification of life as a single, monstrous, planned structure. No matter what we may do, our plans and tendencies are transformed in this direction under our very hands. No matter what course we may think we are following, we infallibly revert to this one point of the compass. The world revolution is our fate. The more we think we are opposing it, the more surely we are helping it to victory. The political temptations and confusions of the age are the means that force us in the very direction from which we strive to escape.

ONLY THE BEGINNING OF THE REVOLUTION

The capitulation in France was something strangely unreal, ghostly. For all those weeks of drama after the invasion of Holland, people waited and waited for the effort that would pull things together again. It seemed as sure as the ups and downs of French history in past centuries.

Nothing came. There were no reserves to strike at the decisive moment; there was no kindling and invigorating force.

Is this the end of France as a great power? Is it the end of her history? Does it not after all represent the verdict upon a political form that was no longer keeping pace with the new reality?

It had long seemed alarmingly likely that Germany would not remain the only country where the middle classes collapsed, and with them the form of democracy governed by persons of rank. It was simply a question of favorable conditions for surrender in other countries as well. Yet this lack of stamina among the masses, of which the middle class must now be considered part, is only one aspect of the problem.

The opinion that actually the old form of democracy has already abdicated is not confined to Fascist circles. Today it is also the belief of the more intelligent younger group that began as socialists. They hold that the drive toward mass leveling of life, and thus the disintegration of all older traditional values, cannot be arrested. The older forms of democracy, they think, make this impossible because there is no longer any firm foundation of agreement, and no ethical standards hold good any more. Therefore they say there is but one thing to do — yield cautiously to this pressure toward total collectivization. It is, they say, only by adroitly manipulated force operating under the screen of mass hypnosis that a small, self-replenishing elite class can still direct the course of events. They are sure that anything else will be fruitless and foredoomed to failure.

This much is certainly true: that the parliamentary form of democracy is always more difficult to work, and that nations unpracticed in its operation are destined for shipwreck. But does this mean that we must come to a new absolutism, and that in order to satisfy the masses we need only tell them that this is their longed-for freedom? Does it mean that we need no longer guarantee freedom, but only security?

Here lies the chief future danger that the revolution will become universal, and that all the revolutionary tendencies of a great totalitarian absolutism will come into one focus. We are only at the beginning of the world revolution, not at the end.

3

The Revolution of Nihilism Is Universal

ABOVE ALL ELSE the revolution is universal. It cannot remain simply European. It is the final phase of the great revolutionary process that has steered the last five hundred years of Western history. There is nothing beyond it — nothing but to return. Not to return in the sense of reaction, not the restoration of medieval conditions or of particular royal houses. It is a return in the sense of a pendulum swinging, starting back in the other direction. The revolution of nihilism is the ultimate form of the autocratic human will to dominate, at the point where it is transformed into its own opposite: serfdom and bestiality.

Perhaps this development was bound to come because only some such final extreme consequence could force a return. Only this consequence can reveal what was destruction even in the French Revolution, and show why the Communist revolution, so long prayed for, was bound to take some form such as the Bolshevik uprising. There are special reasons why Germany was the country where this ultimate experiment became a historical fact. But the question whether the whole world must pass through a phase of revolutionary nihilism, or whether it can be spared this, is surely the one significance of the present war, as well as the subject of deeper reflection upon the nature of the world crisis.

The danger of general infection is great. There is no remote corner of the earth, no nation that does not carry within it the germs of revolution. The curative forces require clear recognition of the disease's symptoms before they can take effect. These forces exist in our vast, as yet unexhausted, cultural heritage. They are not magic powers, and there are no wizards to wield them.

THE REVOLUTIONARY CONTAGION

The dynamite with which Hitler has blasted his way to the nerve center of the democracies' will-power consists of a few absurdly simple ideas. He has contrived to mislead socialist society by his slogan that this is a capitalist war in which the socialist is not concerned; his time is yet to come. He has paralyzed the propertied classes with the slogan that war is bound to destroy property. If the war is carried through to the end, he says, nothing can be more certain than the thing it was supposed to avoid, namely the communism of universal pauperhood. The masses will rule, and total dictatorship will be the inevitable end. To the politically inert masses Hitler has given the only catchwords that ever attract them —"Why war?", "Rejoice in life," "Strength through joy," "Happiness, peace, security." Peace could be assured tomorrow; it would be here today if the people had the last word, if the common sense of the man in the street could prevail against the politicians. He, Hitler, is himself a man of the masses, and that is how he claims he has won the heart of the German man in the street. It is the bigwigs who complicate matters. Everywhere it is the same type who juggles the little man's money out of his pocket, and his life away from its everyday comfort.

Hitler addresses himself to a third class. These are the adventurous, the restless, those with too much energy. For them he has on tap the obsolescence of the European order, the weariness of an outworn civilization, the attenuation of a bourgeois and Christian age long since dead. The strong man must rule, the weak man must serve. Did not Nietzsche say so — has not this been the secret of all vigorous and creative ages? The new age demands new concepts and new tables of laws. It is no longer languages that distinguish among men and states; race alone decides whether one belongs to the new ruling or serving class. A new European nobility, that of the forceful man of action without conventional hesitations, will carve the face of the new Greater Europe.

Most important of all, however, is yet another class that Hitler addresses, though perhaps not directly. I mean the progressives, the advocates of rational planning. It is paradoxical but true that Hitler draws even them into his sphere of influence. Hitler as an advocate of sensible progress, which simply cannot be halted, has a rather odd sound. But is not Hitler actually clearing away obstacles to a reasonable new international order? What, after all, does this multiplicity of European states mean, what these unnumbered economic boundaries, this artificial protectionism? Is there any sense in dozens of national state sovereignties in an age when technology has shrunk distances to nothing? Is not life bound to fight relentlessly onward? Is it not a sign of barrenness and stupidity to oppose the new age through sentiment and resentment, instead of throwing in with the advancing future, and lending a hand?

For a hundred and fifty years past, everything signifying rational order, planning, centralization, uniformity and concentration has enjoyed a reputation for timeliness and progress, as against that which is backward, unorganized, and traditional. How then can that which National Socialism does so remarkably, this monstrous concentration and centralization, this organizing and planning, fail to impress everyone who cannot see the future of the world except in the form of efficient, great machines? Hitler's race doctrine may be absurd, his policies infamous, his method of propaganda insipid, but still the man is marching in the van of the present irresistibly advancing age. Therefore it would be well to come to terms with him, instead of working against him and against the times. There is no question that this argument is often heard, and in extremely intelligent company at that.

This does not exhaust the many tongues in which National Socialism speaks to special groups. We have the psychoanalyst who is impressed by National Socialism's effort to rid itself of the dark side of civilization. We have people accustomed to thinking exclusively in biological categories, and willing to accept the fact that dynamism alone accords with the laws of life, whereas any static order indicates exhaustion of the vital forces.

It is ideas, not facts alone, that play the decisive part in the present struggle for a new order. Production statistics, armament balances and raw-material balances are not the only essential factors in the great conflict. There are also the paralyzing and dividing ideas that have prevented sufficiently prompt resistance to the revolution, and have brought it its partisans all over the world.

How, it will be asked, can you parallel the National Socialist revolution with the great French Revolution, which gained its ends by ideas of liberty and equality? Certainly there is no substantial parallel between the two movements. But they do coincide in that both the revolution of nihilism and the revolution of the rights of man pretended to be a new order of things irresistibly establishing itself in opposition to an *ancien régime*. Here is the card that is played with each class in its own special way, plausibly and strikingly. This is what gives Hitler his undeniable superiority over his adversaries. As the political force of the present revolution, National Socialism keeps reappearing in a thousand propaganda guises, posing as the force of the new and young in contrast to the inert, the old, the sterile. The potentates of National Socialism never weary of pointing out that new world empires and new social orders can arise and survive only with new dominant ideas. The hundred million allies in all the nations of Europe will not decide the struggle — not unless they are inspired by one great, common idea of a world order different from the one National Socialism offers them. This new order must be not merely equal but superior in force of will, ethical standards and clear conception. And it must be equal at least in the greatness and breadth of the universal solution with which it can oppose the will to total world domination.

THE REDEMPTION OF DEMOCRACY

The point most characteristic of the relationship between an *ancien régime* and rising new revolutionary forces is the old order's lack of confidence in the effectiveness of its own weapons, and its overestimation of the unknown impact of the revolution. We have in consequence a policy of soothing and diverting the revolutionary forces instead of confronting them sharply and energetically at the start of their career. The *ancien régime* lacks any real instinct of self-preservation. It has lost the sure sense inherent in every vital organism for what will be advantageous or harmful to itself. Every *ancien régime* characteristically loses its sense of proportion, its eye for the important and the insignificant. It overestimates trifles, and overlooks the real motive forces that confront it. The *ancien régime* is easily disconcerted. Therefore what it does against the forces of innovation is usually wrong. It is arbitrarily harsh where true assimilation of the new elements is necessary, and it goes to the point of entire capitulation and surrender of important rights where stubborn resistance is called for.

It is typical of declining regimes that their decisions are wavering and contradictory. Emotional paralysis and bewilderment characterize their attitude. It seems better to do nothing than to risk doing something wrong. In the *ancien régime* all willingness to assume personal responsibility disappears. There are sudden and baseless alternations between unjustified optimism and light-mindedness on the one hand and black pessimism on the other. The *ancien régime* is fertile soil for a multitude of rumors,

28

for every sort of tale-bearing. Skepticism hides behind an outward loyalty to recognized authority. Irresistibly the concepts and standards of the revolutionary forces penetrate the thinking of the *ancien régime,* gradually transforming it from the ground up. Finally the feeling becomes general that there is no use: the current of development is simply not to be dammed. Something like predestination is at work, and at best one may personally dodge the blow. Developments inherent in the logic of the situation cannot be opposed.

Eventually all comes to a head in the resolution to capitulate and try at least to save for oneself whatever can be saved. One man may do so with little, another with much personal dignity, but inevitably everyone must face the facts. Anybody who does not is either a fool, and deserves his fate, or a blunderer, and must pay the price of his blundering. And he who resists out of conviction is ridiculous. In the *ancien régime* there are no such things as convictions. It is the sign of all abdicating powers that they have lost the feeling for their own rights, exchanging them for an amused skepticism toward all human values.

There is a great similarity between the relation of the democratic powers to National Socialism, Fascism and Bolshevism, and the relation of any Western *ancien régime* to new revolutionary forces. I do not assert that the democracies are abdicating powers, but I believe one may truthfully say that they have long behaved like abdicating powers.

The secret of Hitler's success against his opponents in Germany as well as his foreign adversaries is his wily use of the psychological inferiority attaching to an *ancien régime* as against a revolutionary force. National Socialism plays all the way up and down the scale of emotions from confusion to total paralysis, to the feeling that all resistance is useless. It is always the aggressor, and it is also always the representative of the new, the coming, the vital elements as against the old, senile, ossified.

Recent developments in France bear witness to the speed with which it gains belief for this presentation of itself. The coin issued by National Socialism passed current in all camps. Its expressions and concepts were handed on, became established, and so consequently did its ideas and standards of value.

From "living-space" to "right of young nations" and "new world order", a torrent of new National-Socialist-coined parallels pours into the defenseless, passive and inert political thinking of the democratic states, slowly but basically transforming their entire intellectual and political life. All these processes are much more complicated and far-reaching than the comparatively crude effects of fifth columns and paid auxiliary forces. The disintegration of the self-preservation instinct in the nation attacked remains impalpable; it is not an act that can be punished by law. It is not defeatism, it is the complete inner transformation of the victim; long invisible, it comes suddenly and astonishingly to light.

The mysterious part of this process is the parasitically induced change in the will to live, the blindness toward one's own true interests — blindness toward the mortal dangers that surround one, sometimes even including the morbid sense of well-being and fatuous trust in the future so characteristic of moribund personalities.

Here are dangers that it is not too late to call attention to. But only ruthless and fearless scrutiny of the real situation can save the day. All the mistakes that we in Germany made with and in respect to National Socialism are being made again in other countries. They rest on half-thinking, on false optimism, and a complete misapprehension of the entire situation. They depend above all on the employment of concepts and standards of judgment familiar to us but no longer in accord with the new circumstances.

4

The Very Heart of This War

THE SHOPS ARE FULL; bustling crowds fill the streets. Seemingly everyone is concerned with the moment, not thinking of the events that draw near from yonder, across the Channel. But the truth is different. This is only the protective coloring of an attitude that has remained healthy and straightforward. The people are settling down and preparing themselves to assume the burden of their destiny — a grievous and utterly uncertain destiny.

No recriminations are heard, no clamor for the guilty ones makes headway. Everyone scents the mortal danger. For two or three weeks you could feel the hidden worry. There was no paralysis, but a convulsion down to the roots of existence; then things started upward with unparalleled vigor, endurance, ready subordination to the laws of necessity.

The chance to live in these days in this country and this city is a privilege. One can feel its healthy spirit penetrating his own skin. Here and here only destiny may turn. We shall be witnesses of its decision, which will hold for many generations to come.

But it is plain that the real nature of the war is still not understood. Is it a war at all? Is it not rather the universal revolution itself? The military part is incidental, or at least secondary. It is a means to an end. This is not a war like the one twenty years ago or those in the middle of the last century, let alone in the classical times of Marlborough. Overwhelming as military operations may be, they are all mere spectacle, mere externals; the essential part goes on in secret, remote from public view. Military operations in the present struggle have the no doubt very important function performed by the pursuit after old-fashioned battle, namely complete annihilation of the enemy's strength after it has once been shaken. The emphasis is on "once shaken." This shaking was the purpose of the political battle of revolutionary disintegration that went before.

It is possible to withstand pursuit after losing a battle, as many instances in the history of war go to show. It is even possible to transform a lost battle into a victory by such resistance in an apparently desperate situation.

Certainly Hitler has succeeded to a very great extent in his preliminary weakening. He has won the first battle. This must be recognized, and it is necessary to go further, and realize that the battle consisted of a political and revolutionary shock.

Hitler has carried out exactly what he hinted even in 1932, before his seizure of power. But the emphasis in what he has accomplished is not on such phenomena as parachute troops or fifth columns or Quislings. These are means of accomplishment, nothing more and nothing less. The real piece of work is the deliberate misleading, division and paralyzing of the whole nation — a job for whose success there is one great elementary requirement: the latent pre-revolutionary condition which all the elements favoring order in the various nations are now in.

A healthy, vital democracy could no doubt be beaten at arms, but not so utterly shattered as France was. The material weapons may have been so overwhelming that resistance was impossible. But the important point is why this material superiority existed, why a healthy nation did not take the necessary defensive measures beforehand. Hitler's part in destroying the external order consisted in exploiting an already paralyzed will to live. If it had not been for the pre-revolutionary condition his political acrobatics would have been fruitless; without the flagging of a healthy spirit of resistance he could never have built up so much better a war machine. The nations that have succumbed to him had the germs of destruction already within them. Hitler could indeed render the bacteria virulent, he could create the fever that hastened dissolution, but first the body must have been attacked and its resistance weakened.

Even for Hitler this revolutionary decomposition was at first but a military expedient. Unquestionably he had originally intended nothing more than to facilitate or replace military operations by political means. He did not begin as the world revolutionary he is today. He and his generals started with the example of Ludendorff and Russia. Out of an improvisation in 1917, when the German General Staff let Lenin and Trotsky into Russia, there was created a system, a doctrine, an extension of strategy.

But now the case is different. The military expedient took on chief importance. The revolutionary operation by which it was

35

intended to force the German people under a new military discipline began to follow its own laws. It did so because in Germany there existed a pre-revolutionary situation where all the orderly elements were eaten away. It grew out of its inventors' and advocates' hands; the revolution became the main thing, subordinating to itself both military and economic aspects. The people's entire life swept into a dizzy process of transformation.

The whole war turns on these two points — its core is the revolution, and the revolution moves forward continuously, irresistibly. It moves irresistibly because the nations themselves, already in a state of quasi-revolutionary upheaval of their economic, political, social, and spiritual lives, draw near it from one or the other direction.

THE LIMITS OF THE MILITARY ASPECT

Gigantic though the demands for military action are, the military leaders must get used to the idea that it alone can never win the war, indeed cannot even suffice for defense. Perhaps this war can be won in a military way, only to be lost politically in far greater degree than was true of the last war. For instance would not this be the case if the nihilist and revolutionary elements in the new tyranny should come to dominate the victor too, determining his character for the future?

We are in the midst of such a movement. The danger of military operations being ineffective is twofold. Not merely because the revolutionary core in the great mixed enterprise of the present war is overlooked, but because people allow the revolution to impose its law of action upon them.

36

Nothing could be more mistaken than trying to combat the world revolution by the same revolutionary methods that it uses itself. This attempt has already failed in Germany. It simply rendered the revolution itself more radical. Nothing could be more ineffectual than to acquire a machinery of domination and direction similar to that possessed by the totalitarian tyranny.

But what *is* necessary is to grasp the new reality whence the revolutionary powers have derived their temporary superiority — the new technical, political, economic, and also the psychic reality; and above all the psychic and intellectual reality that the totalitarian powers have managed to exploit.

Without military stamina, indeed, all other resistance is nothing. But this time we cannot allow the political goosequill warriors to lose what the soldiers have won. The military men will gain mere shadow victories unless they realize that their operations are but part of a vast whole.

THE ROAD INTO THE NEW WORLD

It has all grown unreal. After a night like this it is only with difficulty that you find your way back to everyday civilian life. What else counts but just this one thing, resistance?

In the last war the man at the front lived a life subject to its own laws, apart from the civilian world. The world of peace, hope, familiarity lay far behind him, unreal in the shadows. There was no conflict with it. Today the hardest task of all is to harmonize civilian and military worlds — again and again, daily, hourly.

This nation is possessed of a natural wisdom. It declines to anticipate, and so conserve its full power of resistance and capacity for recuperation in real danger. It has a closer union of instinct and reality; it is nearer to nature than we Continentals, despite the outwardly metropolitan and industrial character of its civilization.

Sociability has become a hard task, but a salutary one. It is astonishing how universally people maintain their calm. Not a sign of panic, nervousness, or even of conversation about damage done. One night I was going home by taxi through dark streets; there was fire spouting from the mouths of the guns through the trees in the square. As I was counting, a bomb dropped on the square a hundred yards away. We were at the front, no doubt of it.

Nevertheless, even in the days yet to come the foresight of common sense will lag behind actual events. It is easy to be suspected of panic-mongering if one points out the things that already stand forth on the horizon as future phases of the revolution, nay as probabilities. Hitler will leave no weapon unused, especially not when his star begins to wane. He will not retire, resigned; he will try to drag a world with him to his own downfall, and perhaps to bring about the "Twilight of the Gods" that he loves so well. Somehow he seems to feel even today that there is nothing left for him but to live forever as the greatest destroyer in history. It may also accord with his own innermost unconscious desire — with his soul, afflicted, despite all his successes, with a weariness of and dislike for civilization.

No imagination can paint the horrors of destruction that are being prepared with calculating cruelty even now. The chemical plants in Germany are working feverishly on poison gases. Factories are manufacturing gelatine capsules in which living bacteria cultures lie ready for epidemics. According to a truly diabolical plan the seaports and vessels of Great Britain are to be infected so that, owing to the quarantine, they can enter no foreign port, and thus the blockade will be complete. Of course you cannot do both — infect the British Isles with pestilence and at the same time occupy them. But you *can* try to infect them because you cannot occupy them. Islands are suited to the process — and remote continents. Perhaps these anthrax bacilli and dysentery and typhus germs, being bred today as domestic animals were in happier times, are meant for America.

Today all this may still be considered a figment of the imagination, just as the assault on the American Continent is. National Socialism may perhaps shortly offer pledges and proofs of its friendly disinterest toward the United States. It is sure to happen, despite all the experiences of other states with such pledges, that there will be large groups who believe in them, because this credulity is useful or comfortable. For this belief in a "separate Europe" and a "separate America" there is but one cure: to realize the true character of the threat.

Hitler and his men knew that the world was in a stage of monstrous transformation. This transformation could be hastened or retarded. It could bring revolutionary catastrophe. A universal world revolution offered a chaos for Germany to become the leading world power, and in turn for a new class of ruthless realists inside Germany.

In his beginnings Hitler dwelt amid the notions of the Pan-Germans and German Populists. He believed that in the succession of nations called to world dominion Germany would follow

Great Britain, as Great Britain had followed ancient Spain. In the growing revolutionary tension of the world situation he saw his unique opportunity to achieve this domination. He was convinced that only world revolution would bring Germany to leadership among the powers. Therefore it was his task to drive this world revolution forward, and as it were to put on his payroll the destructive and disintegrating forces in all nations.

The unique, great advantage of the German leaders over other powers and personalities consists in their early recognition of the rising world revolution, and in their ability to exploit it. Even the old rationalistic German politicians never saw anything but "crises" with one eye, and "bright spots" on the horizon with the other. Hitler, on the contrary, knew there was more at stake than business depression, markets, raw materials or boundary revisions. But he had also grasped something more, and if he did not recognize it himself, his friends helped him to recognize that only the nation that wins the mastery of the seas can really rule the world. This means the great open ocean, not what the Germans call seas, the Baltic or the North Sea. Hitler, as an Austrian inlander who had never so much as seen salt water until quite late in life, thought in continental terms. To him the sea is alien, uncanny; he does not love it as he does the mountains, and he has never become intimate with it. Nevertheless he is convinced of the truth that a world power must dominate the great oceans, and he has realized that a new world dominion can arise only through the collapse of the old.

5

The Seafaring Democracies

THAT IS SOMETHING we must know if we are to understand Hitler's true relation to Great Britain. At least for the past decade or so, Hitler has left no doubt that Germany could not become the dominant world power unless England's power were destroyed. But Hitler's offers of compromise with England were genuine to this extent, that he did not wish a military conflict with England, let alone with the whole Empire. He considered it the cardinal error in the policy of the German Empire that things ever reached the point of war between the rising and the dying world power. For, he and his intimates argued, the war had temporarily regenerated England, and simply delayed the process of dissolution instead of hastening it. Any new war would merely strengthen once more the English people's will to survive, and it might have the effect of a second regeneration instead of final destruction. For that matter a war with the Empire would be ticklish from a military point of view. The Empire, they felt, had many resources of strength that could not be accurately estimated beforehand. At best one might take up the struggle with the British Isles alone, but never with the whole Empire, in whose train the United States was bound to appear as an adversary sooner or later.

THE TEMPTATION OF GREAT BRITAIN

It was necessary then, Hitler reasoned, to dissolve Great Britain from within, to bind it by alliances to National Socialist Germany, to transform it inwardly, corrupt it, cause it to degenerate. This is the meaning of the celebrated junior partnership between Great Britain and Germany, this the purpose of Hitler's costly efforts at alliance. It seems to me that if we recognize this part of Hitler's policies, Ribbentrop's mastery of intrigue must appear in a rather doubtful light. Perhaps it is not too much to say that if Germany had had another ambassador, say a man more of the old school, in London, Hitler might have succeeded better in preserving peace for another six months; and then if he had shown a little more moderation and a less intransigent attitude in the Polish question, his plans might possibly have worked after all. The tendencies toward coming to a compromise with Germany were as strong as that.

Is it fortunate for Great Britain that war came? This is a question I do not care to answer. Yet for the future of Great Britain and the Commonwealth the question has never been greater than when there was still a possibility of compromise with the present German system of world revolution. Hitler committed the decisive blunder of his life when for the sake of a showy triumph he threw away a possible success, though one that would not have produced such theatrical results. How he was induced to do this against his better judgment is unknown. Perhaps Ribbentrop, of subaltern mentality and limited capacity despite all his slyness, managed to convince Hitler that he need not go the long way around to destroy the Empire — that England was too decadent even to venture a war.

Hitler's original intention of eating away the British power from within parallels to some extent his tactics toward the conservative forces in Germany itself. He made his pact with them in 1933, only to push them to the wall within a year or two despite the pact. The feat he accomplished here was certainly no less surprising than a similar dislodgment of Great Britain from its spheres of sovereignty would have been if he had managed to form his junior partnership.

But Hitler's attempts to conquer England from inside were by no means concluded with the outbreak of war. On the contrary: they are simply about to begin in a new way. To call this a war of nerves or a psychological war is feeble language indeed. It is not hard to follow the considerations that guide Hitler in breaking up the national unity of an adversary from within. In his opinion there is no unified national will to survive under a democratic or liberal regime. There are nothing but interests and complexes of aims, easily played off one against another.

The English masses, Hitler says to himself, are no better than the modern masses in any industrial country. They have a desire for security, that is, for peace, for the enjoyment of life and recreation, that is, for a better standard of living. They can easily be convinced that the war must infallibly lower their standard of living. As soon as they are shown the uselessness of their sacrifices and self-denial, they will grow refractory. The invariable mistrust of the masses toward any individuals held up to them as leaders, no matter whether from their own ranks or from elsewhere, can be used to explode the body politic. Enthusiasm dies away; mass patriotism is the most ephemeral thing in the world. One may make sacrifices for a time if one is shown why every day. But if time drags on, and the sacrifices threaten to become meaningless, any crowd tends to collapse. These are the reflections that today have led with brutal forthrightness to the bombing of the laboring population in the great English industrial cities. Any populace, Hitler would add, that is not gripped like the Germans or Italians in the iron vise of totalitarian national discipline with its terrorism, is going to become rebellious in a situation like this, where it is losing its all. In a democracy the people can force the government to capitulate. Even at a moment when sure victory is already within reach of that government, rebellious masses can still snatch it away.

Germany is not the field for new revolutions; the democracies themselves are on the eve or actually involved in revolution. Just as the German war economy with all its rationing, derided only recently as a sign of imminent collapse, is introduced now, but inadequately and too late; so too perhaps the democracies will apply National Socialist methods of national discipline. But they will never have the courage nor the power to resort to the one means that will keep the masses docile even in extreme situations: terror and blind obedience. Accordingly, Hitler argues, the British people like the French must sooner or later become fed up; it will then give ear to the voices which have long been trying to show that National Socialism is fighting not the people, but only

their old regime. He thinks, therefore, that he, Hitler, will succeed in convincing the masses that this is not an old-style war of
conquest, but a new world order — the very thing that the English
and French democracies talked of but could never make the German people see.

Furthermore, Hitler will go on to deduce, all the groups with
which until recently he was in such close intellectual contact, and
which believed his promises that Germany had no real designs on
Great Britain, still exist. They believed his assertion that both
states could exist peaceably side by side, the British Empire and
Greater German Europe. The two together would even have the
mission of establishing order in and leading the world.

Then why war, if the two nations are complementary? Why
fight when France has deserted, and the old order of sovereign
national states in Europe is so definitely done for? Why is England still fighting in Europe? Should she not feel relief at being
quit of a nightmare? What do these Continental problems mean
to the British Empire, a great world power with only one foot
planted near the European continent? All the seamen and colonials, used to open spaces as wide as the world, are long since dis-
gusted with this continent sweating in its narrow confines. Is
that anything to fight for? Could not the war have been avoided
by sacrificing France to Germany as she has now sacrificed her-
self? Is not this war sheer folly, and will it not end in total
idiocy? Is it not better to make peace soon, before all parties are
exhausted? Is not the war being fought on behalf of an order in
which nothing we have hitherto lived for will still hold good?
Can this sort of coercive order ever be abolished again? By this

war are we not simply burdening ourselves forever with all the things we wanted to avoid at any cost — planned economy, loss of freedom, totalitarianism, the almighty state, almighty bureaucracy? And are we not losing beyond recall everything we pretend to fight for — freedom and independence, personal initiative and inalienable rights? Will it not plunge us straight into revolution, where no one gains and everyone loses?

Such whisperings as these must be foreseen. From natural reactions of humane anxiety and justifiable hopes the enemy is forging weapons that may be deadly if resisted passively or by unsuitable means. If there are months of a new creeping warfare with a growing decline in all living conditions and constant menace to life and security, then the catchwords that have already hurled one nation from its historic eminence will be handed further. Certainly it will not be the émigrés who do it.

People use the term "traitor," and "paid creature." But the starting-point for Hitler's game is that in these times of crisis no universal rule for determining true interest, honor and patriotism can be found. Hitler exploits the confusion of mind as to what is the vital interest of a class or people, and what only seems to be so. In all ages and countries people are inclined to confuse their own interests with those of society. In normal times the truly general, vital interest stands out above this confusion. Times of great historic crisis, of revolutionary change, on the other hand, are characterized by the fact that this objective sphere is lost. Then arise the dissension and emotional paralysis to which the old regimes fall victim.

Here is the point where Hitler is very sure to develop vigorous activity. First and last the great aim will be to maneuver England out of power. A compromise between Great Britain and Germany would in fact accord with the natural political tendency. Political attempts in that direction therefore are always sure to be met half-way. A real settlement might in truth have meant assurance of world peace for a long time to come. From this it is but a step to ask why the present German regime should be an obstacle to the making of such a pact. What is the distinction among German regimes? None of them is agreeable. They are all fundamentally baffling. It is political realism to reckon with the given quantities, not the desired ones. One must, it is thought, accept the German as he is, and not make the mistake of 1918, when the victorious powers forced the establishment of a democratic regime that proved unable to check the reaction toward an authoritarian, unfree Germany.

Such thoughts will occur the more readily because they have already brought about one decisive change of attitude toward Nazi Germany. The first indignation at the outrages of terrorism and lawlessness, persecution and concentration camps was soon followed by complete indifference. The groups that counted in Great Britain would hear none of them, because they wanted to reach an agreement with Germany. Behind such thoughts as these there is today a further indignation at a France which made bold, after all that had happened, to conclude with Germany a pact that might have preserved the peace of Europe if it had been made earlier and by England.

Could such a pact really have assured peace at any time? I have, so to speak, been making the worse appear the better case.

47

It is therefore necessary to observe that a settlement with the present German regime either before the war or now as a result of it would have meant or would mean the inevitable end of the British Empire. A pact made before the war must certainly have resulted in the dissolution of the Empire; there would have been no stimulation of the recuperative forces that have taken effect at last under the mortal threat of the Germans. This is the very objection that nationalist circles outside the Party made to the National Socialist Leader's war policy even before the war — that by his warlike operations he was obstructing the natural course of development, which must have brought the leadership of Europe to Germany if only war had been avoided.

The destruction of the British Empire is the keystone in Hitler's political arch. It is amazing how sluggish is the imagination of most statesmen, who after all should develop this very gift of putting themselves in their adversary's place in order to forestall his decisions. They do not merely regard as impossible what has never happened before; they will not credit what is perfectly patent, for that very reason — because they think it commonplace or a matter of course. The motives of the coming political war are as unmistakable as those to which France has already fallen victim. It is always the same trick: the men who bring the ill-fated ship of state to disaster never realize that they themselves have long been steered, and are only passing on the catchwords served up to them. Human weakness leads them to take for their own insight what some wily engineer of revolution has already thought for them.

THE TESTING OF THE UNITED STATES

Most people's imaginations are also slow-moving and inadequate in all questions concerning the future of the American Continent. Only the Anglo-Saxon world is capable of vanquishing the revolution of nihilism, and opposing the totalitarian idea of dominion, with its principles of subjugation and terror, the idea of leadership by freely formed public bodies. Both sides have historic origins. Freedom and democracy in England as in the United States are different from what they are on the European Continent, France included. The common elements, but also the distinguishing elements, have been clear ever since de Tocqueville published his great study of the United States. Since Burke's historic fight against the French Revolution it has never been forgotten that democratic freedom in England has little to do with what France won in 1789 by battles, bloodshed and the well-known methods of terrorism, what she then lost, regained, and surrendered once more.

Anglo-Saxon democracy has grown out of a long, consistent history in which there is no definite break. It represents a gradual reshaping of the oldest forms of guild privileges and self-government.

French democracy is its direct opposite in every way. It arose from a break with tradition. The chasm thus opened up to cut off the historical continuity has never been closed. French democracy was a radical innovation. It was doctrinaire and rationalistic. In the idea of rational planning it gave the world one of the supreme political temptations. Here was the beginning of terrorism as a political implement. Here we have the first appearance of the *tabula rasa* idea, the destruction of all organically growing institutions in order to replace the irrational, the historical accretion, with something radically new and reasonable. Jacobinism and the cult of reason made the French Revolution the mother of all the continental revolutions, including the Bolshevist and the nihilist. Through them it was the source of a new absolutism extending into the private sphere, into the very mind of the individual citizen.

The Anglo-Saxon idea of leadership descends directly from medieval institutions of self-government for autonomous bodies and communities. An uninterrupted stream of consistent development runs from the old countries through to the British Commonwealth and the North American Union. Neither Great Britain nor America has what is called a State in the Continental sense. What the Germans before Bismarck understood as the Reich or Realm, in contra-distinction to the Prussian or Austrian State, here survives unchanged to the present day, defying all tendencies toward centralization, bureaucracy and rigid organization. The great strength and the regenerative force, unexhausted even today, of the Anglo-Saxon commonwealth lies in the fact that its organs of self-government have not been turned into machines of domination, but have merely been adapted to modern requirements. Many features that may seem like weaknesses are in reality its very strength. Only in such commonwealths could the attempt be made not to subjugate vast expanses, but to give them the same free forms and educate them to the same free cooperation that had previously seemed possible only in small geographical areas. Men grew up able to lead with a light hand, to scorn tyranny without tolerating whim and chaos.

If any powers are armored against the temptations of totalitarianism it must surely be the Anglo-Saxon countries. Nevertheless they are not. And why not?

The Anglo-Saxon world is capable of being shaken, and has already been shaken to its foundations, because alien ideas and standards have interfered with its own values and old experience, and because it seems to have lost the ability to distinguish between what belongs to it and what is alien to it. To begin with, there is the idea of rational planning, which has come from the world of technology, where it belongs, to intrude on political and social life. If this idea proceeds on the assumption of superiority to all historical accretions — the same assumption every other revolution has made — it too is revolutionary. Rational planning as a principle and not simply as a tool destroys historical values, and interrupts the continuity of development. Where it establishes itself, it prepares the ground for destructive forces.

Secondly we have the new reality of the masses, the fluctuating, unstable, rootless masses. Masses not only of the metropolis, masses too in the open country among farmers and settlers, masses in the small towns, in the centers of intellectual endeavor. Wherever the typical mass character becomes universal, all higher values are as good as lost. In their place arises a more primitive emotional pattern characterized by an elementary need for security and a longing for happiness. Only in the last two decades have we recognized to the full what the rise of these masses means, what threats to the whole substance of human civilization it conceals. It, and not simply Hitler's vile assault, is the deadly menace to our civilization. Hitler's attack could not be dangerous until the revolt of the masses offered him new avenues of invasion.

Here is the entering wedge for Hitler's attack on the United States. He may be planning military action sooner or later, but once again his real design is to destroy from within. Wherever efficient planning becomes the supreme science in political leadership, all sound judgment of particular circumstances, their lessons and limitations, disappears. Where the masses push aside the organic local and historical forms, the will to radical upheaval runs riot in the resulting vacuum.

Hitler thinks he sees the signs of a great revolution in the near future for the United States. This belief has given him confidence, and led him to disdain the warnings uttered early and often by men like Fritz Thyssen, that he must by all means gain the sympathy of the United States for the new Germany, and avoid any rupture. The arguments of these statesmen followed a simple line. If Germany could count on the support or toleration of the United States, it would be comparatively easy to win the approval of Great Britain as well. This was the one way of obtaining just and proper German demands without a war, which was certain in any case to be a world conflagration.

Hitler rejected these ideas because he did not consider North America a decisive factor. Hitler did not admire the United States. His feelings were a mixture of haughty disdain and of reluctant respect for their vitality and their economic and technological ability. His disdain, indeed his contempt, was directed particularly at the political system of the States, and also at American life in general, which he considered raw and puerile. Neither North nor South America, he thought, was a finished political and social entity. On the contrary, it would be a long time before solid political and social forms could be arrived at here. Anything might be expected. There were historic events yet in store for the continent. What pretended to be finished form and political life in America was really but a shadow shape that could be over-thrown at will. It seemed highly plausible that for instance a reaction against liberalist, individualistic freedom might produce very sharp discipline and a centralized machinery of state. Once the United States fell into political turmoil, none could predict what the result would be. There might be chaos of long duration, complete breakdown, disintegration of the artificial and only seemingly powerful industrial machine, and thus a new phase of primitive colonial existence that might even lead to rejuvenation, to a return to the land, and to a new, permanent form. National Socialism must therefore endeavor to take firm root in the United States in good time, so as to influence the course of events. The fate of the American continent could not be a matter of indiffer-ence to National Socialism, since there were no longer any isolated areas, no matter how large and economically self-sufficient they might be. He hoped to range the United States on the side of the young nations. This implied the downfall of the present demo-cratic government.

In substance Hitler has repeatedly told his intimates that he was not afraid of the United States as a power because it was his pur-pose to unloose upon the American continent a revolution of un-precedented dimensions. Sooner or later America's hour would strike, to create a new future through breakdowns and turmoil on a gigantic scale. When asked how such an upheaval would be possible, he replied with a wealth of alleged facts of which it was almost impossible to have any real knowledge in Germany. He mentioned the ever-growing uprooted masses, the destruction of the old colonial world with its sharply defined political and social ideas. There was, he said, a vast army of the economically disappointed, the unsatisfied, who have always formed the reservoir for new revolutions everywhere. He said there was a special world of lads completely without hesitations, the world of adventurers and gangsters. There was a not inconsiderable contingent of persons who took pleasure in cruelty and tortures. In the eyes of the National Socialist elite, America was, so to speak, a naked, brutal world where the will to power and ruthless violence was veiled only by a gossamer sheath of convention, which one could rend in a moment. What opportunities for disintegrative propaganda, for the formation of revolutionary organizations! These "bootleggers" and other remnants of prohibition could be hired as mercenaries. There were innumerable creatures ready to do anything for money. The system of the political entrepreneur, the "boss," who deals in votes for money, seemed rather close to National Socialist Party ideas.

And then there were all the national tensions, the contingents of European peoples. They did not become Americans by the second generation, scarcely by the third, but clung to their city ghettos, accessible to any propaganda; or else they lived in the country, and kept up their old connections. They bore within them the most perilous of all burdens in times like these: divided feelings and inner bewilderments without the balance possessed by settled, civilized nations. If even the civilized could be shaken today, and were casting aside their political thinking like an outworn garment, what was to be expected of these immigrants who had not yet established any inner relationship to the political and social concepts of the new world?

Finally there was the lack of a powerful army, of rigorous discipline to counterbalance individualism and unrestrained liberty. Bribery and corruption, by means either crude or refined, seemed to open all doors even on the upper levels of society. The determination to make money regardless was bound to break down barriers that after all had still existed in Germany and the European states, offering initial resistance to the revolution. In America, like other countries, there was such a thing as great ambition, and thus the possibility of buying important men with the lure of conscious patriotism. In view of all the glaring weaknesses and abuses, the cry "America awake!" was bound to take effect. Delivering America and preserving her from disaster might be a good bait for despairing patriots or those who imagined they were.

In Germany, National Socialism owed its triumphant career to the factor referred to as "driftwood." This was the mass of basically non-political persons, uprooted by inflation and war, the economically exhausted and unsuccessful, the humdrum lives without hope, the white-collar workers even more than the proletariat or petit-bourgeois workers. This economic and political, this social and moral driftwood was especially plentiful in America. Space had grown finite within and without; there were no unlimited

possibilities left. The strain was growing; old tensions were rein-
forced by new; the old ones still went on. There was the race
question, the Negro question, the conflict between northern and
southern states, between east and west. Hitler had particularly
great expectations of the race question in America. He believed
that the conflict fought out in the Civil War was by no means
over. As in Germany, he expected the surviving old ideas and
rivalries to have a dividing effect. He thought it feasible to recur
to the old forms of an American commonwealth, in order thus
to win over that part of the nation which today is skeptical of
modern mass democracy, and lives amid dreams of the romantic,
better, more vigorous world of its forefathers.

Above all there was the Jewish question. In view of the large
Jewish element in the cities, and the position of its members in
the American new-rich class, it seemed mere child's play to fan
anti-Semitism, and thus to set off the revolutionary forces, as had
been done in Germany. Jew-baiting, in which the National Socialists have gradually attained a practiced unscrupulousness by no
means fully displayed even in Julius Streicher's paper, is the means
of creating initial propaganda cliques throughout the world. Already now we can realize the part played in the French success by
anti-Semitism, combined with the war on Freemasonry. It was so
in Poland, so in Czechoslovakia, so in Austria. Everywhere anti-
Semitism was the entering wedge for disintegration, for the split-
ting up of the body politic, for the satisfying of economic envy
and the launching of a revolutionary attack on property.

It is not for me to judge how far Hitler's ideas about the United
States may be right or wrong. I want simply to report the back-

ground against which Hitler's political ideas on America matured. Many of the things he said were merely tossed off for the moment, and carried no great weight. Much was the notion of those around him, whom Hitler did not always contradict. It does remain a question of burning importance to the whole world how the American people will react to the menace of the nihilist revolution. It would be a grave misapprehension of the danger to see it simply in airplane and troop invasions or spectacular sabotage.

Such dangers do exist. In the course of this war mechanical resources will be so extended, and the political opportunities may be so favorable, that sooner or later we might just conceivably see America occupied by armed forces from another continent. But here too the real danger lies in revolution, of a kind very different from that applying to Great Britain or France — to wit, not in the sense of one great revolutionary act. The alien ideas, the slogans of the nihilist revolution, which pretends like all revolutions to represent liberation and a new order, are permeating the masses even today. There is no isolation; it has long since broken down. The American continent, all its desires to the contrary notwithstanding, is in the midst of battle. No declarations can keep the American nation from taking sides in the present struggle. For them not to make up their minds, and not to combat National Socialism and its revolution, signifies in itself a decision favorable to the revolution and the support of National Socialist world domination. It has that significance even if one is far from sharing Hitler's arbitrary judgment of the future of the United States, and his confidence that she has only the choice of introducing a dictatorship similar to National Socialism or surrendering to a native form of Bolshevism.

We must not despise Hitler's notions, even though we consider them wrong and reject them. The diabolical thing about the present age is that hysteria and suggestion can produce realities even in the political world — realities that may be described as pseudo-creations, but none the less effective. The state of the collective mass subconscious today is such that it ought to be carefully watched. In that subconscious the false creative forces of hysteria and mass mania lie in wait, ready to conjure up a world whose reality no one capable of judgment could possibly believe in.

If America is the country where the citizen still reaches for his rifle on behalf of freedom, and not simply for his check-book to buy temporary grace from the new revolutionary powers by a suitable monetary contribution, then indeed we may rest easy for the outcome of the nihilist revolution. In her great open spaces America certainly possesses some sort of buffer against attempted rebellion. Possibly there will be only fragmentary efforts in the United States. But the great distances might also serve to protect coups d'état built on Trotsky's pattern with skeleton staff organizations. They might be able to occupy the key positions in a given territory before federal forces could intervene. The material and moral resources of the United States are tremendous; they are perhaps the world's greatest. But they are unorganized; their form does not permit of a united defense. Perhaps the best of the existing organizations on American soil belongs to the very group of the population that is not loyally inclined toward the

official regime of the United States. And in coups d'état and revolutions an organized minority always carries the day against an
unorganized majority.

In addition to the skeleton staffs trained in producing coups
d'état there are also centers, equally well trained, for the circula-
tion of whispered catchwords, for an effective propaganda that
uses neither radio, newspapers, nor leaflets, but persons specially
detailed to spread slogans by word of mouth. These slogans may
be almost inestimably effective. The weapons of psychological
warfare have never been catalogued, nor indeed sufficiently noticed
at all. Here is one of the greatest opportunities for success.

Part II

1

Hitler's Technique Again

HITLER AND HIS ASSOCIATES live in a constant maze of shifting ideas and plans. This is the reason for many conflicting accounts of National Socialist intentions — a reproach, incidentally, held up against my reports as a sign of untrustworthiness. In reality it is quite impossible, with Hitler's technique, for discrepancies of intention not to become public. Hitler is operating upon the United States as he did in Germany and in Austria after he had seized power; he initiates activities at various levels simultaneously, with varying purposes and missions. He always gives plenipotentiary powers to several different men and pressure groups. This is the result of a carefully considered technique that facilitates his camouflage. Hitler can play the groups off against each other; he can disavow one or another, accepting it as part of the bargain that the rival organizations combat one another. Thus Hitler's momentary political catchwords and slogans are always mere symptoms of his work, but not necessarily representative of his real aims.

For still another reason ideas of what Hitler would do if America were after all to oppose National Socialism are bound to be vague and contradictory. His political technique is entirely empirical, experimental. From various directions and with all the resources of conspiracy he keeps feeling his way closer to the problems he considers important. He constantly fills in his conceptions with actual detail. He corrects and adapts himself; and in these efforts there is one thing he certainly is not, a doctrinarian — even though he may cling with remarkable determination or even pig-headedness to a single line that he keeps returning to. For a system as unscrupulous as National Socialism there are many possible ways of keeping North America from taking active part in a war against Germany. It cannot be denied that the slogans now in use are finding their mark. It would be worth careful investigation to find out how far the isolationist repertory of political ideas originated in National Socialist propaganda workshops. National Socialist propaganda always begins with existing ideas, and then by a slight twist and careful alterations manufactures the tools it considers useful.

That there is no longer any Europe worth fighting for; that we must think in continental terms; that the United States is sufficient unto itself, and that Continental European democracy is no longer a reality — these are the cruder patterns for the brakes now being applied. These catchwords grow more dangerous when definite economic interests and scientific statistics are used to bring them close to the understanding and sphere of interest of certain circles. National Socialist disintegration is not simply loud, assertive mass propaganda, but also invariably specialized propaganda adapted to particular groups and personalities, and highly efficient. The effective individual form is found for use through many channels and in many shapes. Such work can not be blocked by general protective measures; it eludes them. There is but one effective remedy, namely to formulate positive aims and ideals of order for oneself with similar effectiveness and individual attention, and to realize them, not merely to shout for them.

The secret in Hitler's work of disintegration is his adroit combination of tempting promises, reasonable considerations that serve to win confidence, and facts that cannot be argued away, which therefore, have the impact of reality. It is quite impossible to overestimate the propaganda value of a few National Socialist ideas that have worked. They do not show that the world may occasionally stand on its head for a change; they prove rather that at many points the National Socialist order rests on the living forces of the present, rudely discarding outworn notions of an economist's and statesman's orthodoxy that limps far behind reality.

There is still the danger that timely forward steps taken under the totalitarian dispensation may cover up other doings that show the dictators' true nature. Thus measures for creating employment or pursuing an unorthodox fiscal policy have had their effect among certain serious adversaries of National Socialism. Social institutions and even foreign adventures have found defenders because they were based on vital needs of modern life, and because people overlooked the misuse of correct premises.

Hitler's catchwords often have a semblance of reasoned progressiveness, taking account of popular and healthy tendencies. They are simple and obvious, as for instance that of a new European order; the ranging of European nationalities in this new order as parts of a superior political body is convincing to any non-European. Mass propaganda attempts to intoxicate and excite the passions; the real individualized propaganda, however, appeals to common sense, attempting to convince, citing arguments. It is astonishing how greatly people underestimate this individual sort of propaganda; they are even slow to recognize it as such at all. Hitler has always realized that in political operations a sharp distinction must be made between individual and mass propaganda.

For instance, a point that has seemed to give some opening for Hitler's work of disintegration in the United States is the economic crisis. Economic and social resentments are the great propaganda reservoirs. How many American citizens still consider democracy precious by comparison with their economic distresses? How many have thrown overboard all standards, want nothing except to make money, and are ready to do anything? When there are no longer any possibilities of economic improvement, the possibility of political opposition still has a certain value as something to hope for.

Hitler's endeavors are directed toward putting out of commission the machinery that regulates the political interplay of parties and opposition. He undertakes to divide the political elite of each country, and fan into intolerance the existing rivalries in any political faction. He puts his trust in a new elite from other circles than those that have hitherto been the leaders — new groups who hope to establish themselves by new political slogans and methods. A rising elite is always tempted to establish itself be-

66

yond removal, by abandoning the existing rules of the political game.

THE NEW ELITE

The displacement of the old elite is the key point of Hitler's political warfare. In Germany he managed by a wily system of violence, corruption, legal persecution and enticement to eliminate within two or three years the elite whom the old German President had charged him to work with and adapt himself to. He even succeeded in dislodging the officers' corps and the Junkers from their positions of influence. The details of this unscrupulous internal struggle are no longer interesting, but the fact that he has adapted those methods of dislodgment to the elite who oppose him in enemy states is very interesting.

It cannot be said that his effort has entirely failed. Compared to this disintegration of the old elite and furthering of new groups, the ideas and activity of fifth columns are relatively unimportant. There need not always be a whole new elite personnel. There may simply be regroupings. The process that he is secretly furthering may result in mingling new and old cliques. The essential thing is to disrupt the existing method of selecting the elite, to discredit them, and cause them difficulties. True, Hitler cannot eliminate members of the old elite outside Germany by bribery as he so successfully did at home. But he can weaken credit and reputation by rumors, gossip, one-sided and unjust criticism. He is sure to find suitable helpers for this business in each country. He need not even pay them. All he need do is start the ball rolling with his arguments.

The general situation makes his work easy. The crisis of democracy is expressed, among other ways, by functional disturbances in the creation and replenishment of the political elite. Intermediate layers have grown up, cliques between parties, between units and organizations in political, economic and intellectual life. It is not alone the rising and waning generations whose impact on the replacement of strength within the elite is felt in normal times. Nor are they outsiders from the fringes of organized society, self-willed individualists; when such people are useful in normal times they are generally assimilated. The fact of a revolution finds expression in this, that new types of individuals join to form the political and social elite; they are persons who normally would never have had a chance to cross the threshold of public notice.

There are two types particularly successful in pushing to the fore by kindling the imagination and the hope of the masses, now beginning to feel insecure — the utopians and doctrinaire intellectuals, and the cynical adventurers, the strong-arm men. It is an infallible sign of approaching crisis when men of this type, who usually remain aloof from public life, begin to penetrate the chinks and cracks in the old cliques of the political elite, demanding to be heard or laying claim to exclusive leadership.

On the other hand every governmental system that has allowed itself to be pushed into the role of *ancien régime* commits glaring blunders in the choice of persons for important offices. Quite the classical index to the character of any *ancien régime* is the fact that the ruling elite distinguishes itself by lack of talent, of will-power and intuition. A selection takes place according to absence of ability and indeed even frequently of character. As a result everyone of ability and character, even though he may belong to the circles from which the ruling elite is drawn, joins the opposition, and begins demanding the removal of the elite *in toto,* along with the rules and institutions that govern its selection.

Consequently the old elite are hard pressed even from a quarter that would loyally support them in normal times. In the maturest form of democratic life, in England, the contrast between a regime of "old men" and the pushing, rising masses, with their wealth of initiative, has been sublimated as a fruitful force in public life. Only in young democracies without experience of the rules of the game, like Germany — young yet also senile, skeptical, and cynical — does this contrast serve to disrupt the political order. In revolutionary times the case is different. Then, even in practiced democracies, the ruling elite begin to think of dealing with the new difficulties, the rising opposition, by creating as it were an irremovable elite. Not only the weapons of the party machine are used to shut up disagreeable opponents, but the weapons of the state.

This starts off a vicious circle of mistakes and misapprehensions that ends with all the groups demanding an irremovable position of authority. There is a sort of race for the positions of power, from which people "refuse to be dislodged." Once this development starts, the revolution is in full swing; it can no longer be halted. And thus an unscrupulous foreign power with large intellectual and material means at its disposal finds it comparatively easy to use the group rivalries in order to disintegrate and manipulate the entire nation.

THE NEW ELITE IS NOT REMOVABLE

It is the unadmitted worry or hope of every political party in present-day democracy that the modern elite, once they attain power, will be hard to get rid of. This is a new factor among political realities. Orderly change and the possibility of removing the elite if necessary are no longer taken for granted in politics.

There are two reasons for this. Owing to the resources of modern propaganda and the rise of the great masses, political leadership is more and more precariously preserved from chance demagogic majorities and disastrous decisions. On the other hand the instruments of power belonging to the modern state are so overwhelmingly effective that the group controlling these instruments can scarcely be forced to surrender them.

This means that political battles are fought on very shaky ground. At any moment one party may violate the conventions on which the interplay of political forces depends, and thus abruptly we have what is euphemistically called an authoritarian regime, but what must actually be called modern absolutist tyranny. The question on everyone's lips is, how long can a modern political party or elite withstand the temptation to abuse the resources of modern state power once it possesses them?

In the new leader-dominated states there is no way at all to replace one elite with another. This means not merely that the first cliques to seize the modern implements of power and use them with determination simply cannot be removed, and thus are beyond all effective criticism; but also that there is a surreptitious race to see which group shall first discard the old rules of parliamentary democracy and profess its adherence to the new political reality.

Each group may very well honestly believe it is acting not for itself and its private interests, but for the future of the nation, or liberty, or socialism, or a new order, or whatever its goal happens to be. One is more likely to do for the sake of a general ideal what one would not dare to do in public, confessedly for oneself.

I do not think it is too much to claim that such considerations had a part in the shift of French policy. But the fears or hopes are quite similar in all the countries that still preserve a democratic life. It may be that someone decides not to surrender the special authority or institutional facilities for modern mass direction originally made necessary by war; or there may be a plan to strike at an opportune moment and install a certain group in absolute power as trustees for new classes of the populace. The virulent poison of mutual mistrust enters political life, because suspicion arises that your political adversary may intend to get permanently ahead of you, capturing power and putting you in the shade indefinitely.

In the present war a secret struggle for power is going on behind the scenes, and this it is that opens great opportunities for outside influence. Even this aside, the hidden wrestling reveals the situation plainly as a world civil war, a universal revolution of which the military war is but one symptom. It is to be suspected that the fronts in this civil war cut straight across all nations in quite another way than people generally realize. It is a mistake to see only the national fronts, which will probably change more than once in the course of the war anyway.

RUSSIA AND THE STRUGGLE FOR A MONOPOLY OF EMPIRE

It is a mistake to think that only democratic regimes can be dissolved or made politically dependent with the aid of rival elite groups. Considering what has gone before, it seems unlikely that Hitler would refrain from using his most effective "secret weapon" on Russia in particular, and confine himself to military means; it would have seemed unlikely even if certain details of his political preparations had not come out.

Of course the political struggle here cannot be carried out along the same lines as seemed promising with the Western European nations. The exploitation of dissatisfied elements in Soviet Russia offered no prospects. And the promotion of special national interests, as in the case of German efforts to create centers of agitation in Ukrainia, rather distracts attention from the main point than provides a serious means of fomenting dissension. To recur to old social classes would be silly. There are only two possibilities for gaining influence from outside — to win the Soviet Army and to win the younger intelligent generation of the Bolshevik elite.

No matter whether the National Socialists ever made an actual attempt in the first of those directions. If they did, it was a failure; it cannot be repeated. But the alternative remains. There can be no doubt that Hitler is attempting it.

In order to understand the real possibility — however preposterous it may seem — of winning over portions of the Bolshevik elite, we must keep in mind the intellectual history of the intelligent, younger Soviet functionaries, particularly the technical officials.

These are young men who do not remember pre-revolutionary times, who believe in nothing but the power of technology, and who regard the doctrines of Bolshevism as unimportant or outworn. Among these younger technocrats and bureaucrats a class has arisen that adheres only to the ideas of efficient planning. They want an order stripped of everything that suggests irrational origins, history, philosophic attitudes; the concepts of nationalism seem as stale as those of bourgeois individual morality.

It is conceivable that Hitler's attempts to make contact with this elite may have some chance of bringing Russia gradually into the German sphere by cooperation from within. No doubt a lengthy process, but not an impossible one from the outset. The only reason it is hard for Hitler is because he cannot wait. But even so it may be that before the war he favored a plan to fit this vast territory peaceably into his scheme for a new order, and assimilate the rising Soviet elite or use them as a tool of his own.

In any case Hitler will have to wring out a decision on the position of Russia. The great European realm that Hitler plans cannot exist if the Slavic Union goes on as an independent and self-contained political order. It is customary today not to count Russia as part of Europe. But such standards of judgment are no longer adequate.

There is more than the Ukraine at stake. A glance at any atlas will show that the geographical transition from Central Europe to the East is just as vague as the ethnographic transition. The present state of things cannot produce a lasting balance so long as part of the Slavic peoples belongs to the Europe of Hitler and another part to the Soviet Union. And the possession of the Baltic as well as of the vitally important Balkans will always be disputed so long as an independent Soviet Union exists. Wherever Germany can lay claim to petroleum it is a threat to Russia; for Germany the oil is not effectively secured until the territories are permanently and indisputably in German hands.

The East's masses of humanity, with their vast fecundity — inexhaustible in comparison with Western and Central Europe — are also important. In military matters Hitler is a pupil of Ludendorff. To Ludendorff the crushing of the Russian steamroller was *the* great German achievement of the World War, and might, properly exploited, have saved not merely Germany but the world from a dreadful nightmare. What the West calls the Pan-Germanic peril is overshadowed by the coming, irresistible Pan-Slavic peril, allied with a Pan-Asiatic threat. Thus ran the arguments of such German men and generals as General von Hoffmann, who continued to imagine even after the German defeat in 1918 that Germany must be allowed to annihilate the new Soviet Union for the protection of Europe and a really permanent peaceful order.

Russia belongs to Europe, and its Asiatic hinterland is a great new pioneer area for all the European peoples, who must not allow themselves to be crowded out by the Mongols. What prospects for the venturesome and restless of all the continental European nations who cannot or will not enter the Anglo-Saxon world! What opportunities if these territories were not dominated by the Russian government, but could be used for the common advantage of all the Central and Eastern European nations, and transformed into huge pioneer settlements and resettlements! These are the popular notions among National Socialist officials, just as they were with the politically-minded generals in the World War. Russia is not an ethnic unit. The thing to do is to Europeanize Russia by dividing it into its ethnic elements and ruling it accordingly. Hitler holds these ideas in slightly different form, but fundamentally they are pretty much the same. There is a book by no less a person than Fridtjof Nansen on Siberia as the land of the future. Hitler has used some of the ideas from the book in his own way. He regards the European continent and the North Asiatic plain as a single major area. Vladivostok to Flushing in Holland — this is not merely the conception of a "primary space" that German Nationalist propagandists are spreading about, but Hitler's goal as well. And it is a goal not so entirely beyond the bounds of possibility as the devotees of custom and tradition may think.

Why should it not be possible to establish an efficient order in an area of this size by a mighty will and the new technique of organized cooperation? Does not the planned economic adjustment of Europe as one great unit demand the complement of a territory so vast and so rich in raw materials? I have heard Hitler dreaming aloud about what a country like Siberia could become under German sovereignty and with purposeful management — a new Canada, a new kind of America with space for settlement, with elbow-room; a country where sensible planning would prevent capitalist devastation and exploitation from the start. Hitler spoke of Russia as an artificial structure that had lost its excuse for existing, quite aside from its Bolshevist government. It is true that in utterances of this sort Hitler likes to embellish his ideas with such historic and romantic themes as Rurik, the Nordic founder

75

of Russia, and his successors. When he says that only Nordic Germans can bestow a new state order upon this vast country, he is simply presenting his ideas in a dress suited to the comprehension of his associates; but the essential part is seriously meant, and should be taken seriously.

Instead of waging a bloody war to the finish with Russia, it is not impossible to form an alliance, a living partnership, and build up the two nations together. Why should not the two unions, the German-European and the Soviet Russian, be able to build a large-scale federation by setting up common headquarters and unified administration? One obstacle is the difference in social and educational level; the Bolshevik elite would have reason to fear being crowded out of all important positions and relegated to a secondary role. But this very point should induce part of the technological elite to range themselves with the superior leading class, in order to participate in it. Is it really true, as is so often asserted, that Stalin desires to make use of German intelligence and organizing ability for the permanent stabilization of Russia? If so, there would be little to prevent such a unification of the great Eurasiatic continental area.

Be that as it may, Hitler is certainly bound to destroy Russia as an independent center of power outside his own Greater European Empire. The inherent consistency of events will compel him to. Hitler cannot keep his subject peoples in line for generations by Gestapo and armies of occupation. He can do only one thing if he is to make his domination "permanent for the next thousand years," namely what he is already beginning to do — concentrate all the implements of power, monopolize all institutions representing power. The industrial machine, along with armaments, is an indispensable condition of the power potential. It must therefore be monopolized. In the future there can be no industry in Europe but German industry. The same thing is true of raw materials, of power, of transportation. Here the giant monopolies of total domination will develop; only by these monopolies can National Socialism hope permanently to control the huge expanse of its European territory.

Can there exist at the same time another order building up the same monopolistic machinery, and in addition considerably richer in human fecundity, fertility of soil, raw materials and area? From this standpoint there is room in the Eurasiatic territory for but one monopoly empire. The two must either wind up in a fight to the finish for sole power, or arrive at a sort of symbiosis, a biological partnership. Within the domain of this order there cannot be an interplay of free forces and self-sustaining bodies and members, but only one central power, in possession of all key points and monopolies.

PARTNERSHIP

What will become of the rest of the world if Hitler succeeds in vanquishing Great Britain? Canada will fall to North America. What will become of Australia and New Zealand?

Hitler's utterances on that point have been few and contradictory. In so far as it is possible to reconstruct his opinion, he is undecided whether the continent should be surrendered to the Japanese or whether it could be made part of a German dominion, and so retained for the white race. If the latter were possible, it could be only under German leadership and with German settlers. Hitler enjoys thinking about the recapture of the former Oceanic island kingdom (part of which has become a Japanese mandate), and the possession of New Guinea and the Dutch territories in the East Indies. But he has also expressed the opinion that all colonial aims must take second place; the most important thing being to gain the friendship and support of Japan. What may happen later cannot be foreseen.

Hitler appeared insufficiently familiar with the problem, but his undeniable instinct for power told him that like the British Empire he must have bases for his domination everywhere. Ubiquity is part of world dominion. One of his oft-repeated maxims on foreign policy was that you must be on hand everywhere, making claims, never really declaring yourself disinterested anywhere. As the *nouveau riche* studies his wealthy neighbor in order to copy his style of living, so Hitler has studied the British world power in order to draw a few conclusions. The most important of these was that a ruling nation must send out its own nerve fibers and muscles across continents and oceans. Hitler forced himself to admit this in spite of his own nature, which is restricted to mere continental conceptions.

Africa, on the other hand, is part of a territory that Hitler can imagine in full perspective. In his eyes it belongs irrevocably to Europe, as the southern part of the American continent belongs to the aggregate continent. Here he was early at work with ideas of an Italo-German division of interests. No matter whether or not it was honestly meant. In the beginning he was basically interested only in the central and southern parts of the continent.

It was one of his favorite colonial ideas to capture for Germany not only Southwest and German East Africa, rounded out with Belgian, French and Portuguese territory, but above all the former Boer country and the old Cape Colony — in other words South Africa. His alleged dislike of colonial possessions was only a means to an end — to get Great Britain on his side during the early days of the German ascent. At that time his attention was concentrated on acquiring a legitimate base in Africa from which he could go on working in his own way, that is, could undertake the confusion, the cleavage and undermining of the political terrain.

The South and Central American situation we can sum up briefly by saying that in his propaganda operations here he relied chiefly on the race problem and the slogan of the right of dominion over colored races and half-breeds — the inequality of man. Recent revelations, however, have shown that this was meant simply for a smoke-screen behind which the real political intrigues could be carried on. Here, too, the aim was to get a foothold on the continent, and pursue operations from there. One single state governed in the German spirit was sure to throw the whole continent into turmoil. There is no practical contradiction in trying to bring the whole southern part of the continent under National Socialist influence and at the same time claiming this territory as the domain of an Italian-Spanish community of interests, so long as the matter in hand is joint preparation for revolution.

By comparison with Africa and America, Hitler adjudged the Far East for the moment a mere means to an end. It is a means

79

of making difficulties in order to weaken Great Britain, breaking down the authority of England and cultivating a belief in the downfall of the British Empire. This is the political line of National Socialism, which here plays the part of honest broker. And indeed the political and scientific institutes founded by Hitler's experts seem to be working not altogether unsuccessfully. He has repeatedly said that his policy here would inevitably force him into inconsistencies. White rule and prestige would be bound to suffer from a struggle between Germany and Great Britain if such a thing should occur. But the rise of the German people to world power justified any temporary loss to the white race. The problems would have to be solved in succession; the lost ground could still be made up.

What Hitler wants in the Near and Middle East is easy to explain today. He finds in these both the key point in the destruction of the British Empire and the all-important petroleum. From here, in league with Italy, he can dominate the entire Mohammedan world.

Partnership is Hitler's trick wherever he thinks he can align forces and nations on his side without having to subjugate them outright. He offered this kind of partnership to Poland; he tried it temporarily with Russia; Italy is a partner of his that will sooner or later have the same experience as his domestic German partner did during the first years of National Socialist rule. Partnership is also his tactical disintegrative weapon against the European and Mohammedan peoples. The liberation and rise to complete sovereignty of all the nations and tribes now under the leadership of Great Britain or France sounds plausible,

and is attractive. A greater Arabia, the union of all the Mohammedan peoples in a great Pan-Islamic Union, the complete sovereignty of Pan-India — these are the catchwords Hitler uses in his
propaganda there. He has expressed his real intentions cynically
but clearly to his own intimate circle.

Despite all experience there are still people who listen to Hitler's siren song, lulling themselves in the belief that what has
already happened to others still cannot happen to them. Why
not go along with Hitler for a while? This is a familiar tune,
originally heard in Germany. The secret of Hitler's success is
something profoundly demonic. Even today, after all that has
happened, Hitler still manages to induce the victims of his drive
for power to submit voluntarily. We have not yet reached the
end of this road of self-delusion.

2

The New Social Basis

WORLD DOMINATION does not mean simply subjugation. World domination requires a new world social order. The two are very intimately connected. If the demand for world dominion is not to remain utopian, mere words, there must be a very special form of domination. The seeming logical impossibility of Hitler's intention to dominate vast territories permanently has deluded many critics of National Socialism into the hope that his rule could not be so bad as all that. Actually it is only here that the poisoned arrowhead appears through the gay feathers of a spectacular world order.

I have found that people hold a personal resentment against me for my report on Hitler's conception of a new social order with a new slave class and a new master class. Why — can there be behind it the hidden thought, never admitted to oneself, that there is an attraction in this idea of Hitler's? Obviously something of the sort must have touched the subconscious of the critics of my Hitler book; in addition there was the alarmed feeling that one should not spread such ideas around, for they were already in the air as it was.

Indeed they are in the air. None other than Nietzsche, so grotesquely overrated by the intellectual snobbery of our German liberals, made the right of the strong over the weak into an outright religion. How strangely fronts shift! What has been blazoned on the banners of intellectual progress in the last fifty years, fluttering like spring into our stuffy Philistine world, is all at once a crime on the part of these same advocates of progress, now that the sun of Hitler has brought glorious summer. It *is* a crime, this that resounds from the new tables of laws, from a veritable anti-Sinai. But it was not Hitler who created the new doctrine of triumph over the rabble by the man beyond good and evil. Nor did Hitler create the universal receptivity to such ideas; it was there long before he began to work. He is doing no more than enjoying the unearned fruits of a revolution in standards of value.

If there were not something basically alluring in Hitler's assault on the civilized world, or if that world, floundering in a period of self-destruction, had not long since grown tired of its humanitarian self-restraint, how could all this have taken practical effect?

I do not believe that any part of Hitler's secret teachings has produced so much inner confusion as the gospel of the masterman and his right to dominion over the colored races of every shade — over weakness. After all, weakness was weak no longer, but had come, in the form of the modern masses, to tyrannize over the world. And the strong individual, the free, creative personality, had become dependent on the masses, and needed protection himself. The revolt of the masses (the new political world

What has changed? The shift is threefold: the technological revolution has so transformed the material basis of our life that the instruments of social regulation belonging to a former age no longer fit it. It has so increased the resources of power as to create an entirely new situation for those possessing that power as well as for those subject to it. It has produced a new phenomenon in human society — masses free from all the restraints of tradition. And lastly our outlook has changed in such a way that even with respect to our inner lives we seem to be in a new world.

The Western outlook has been darkened with strange abruptness. There is going on a puzzlingly violent mental transformation that causes whole series of ideas to vanish without a trace. Insights are simply forgotten, a whole new language is spoken, a new intellectual world comes into being. This is not merely the stage that everyone reaches as he gets older, and begins to see a younger generation with new interests and aims growing up around him, and his surroundings changing. For twenty or perhaps thirty years now the world has been under a new constellation, and events march swiftly. No man can escape the change.

This new thing is at the same time immemorially old. It is the genius of destruction, hitherto banished by civilization from our settled life. It is the urge, suddenly assuming gigantic proportions, to cast off domestication, to be free of civilization once more. It is certainly no romantic Rousseauesque yearning for nature and the primitive; it is like all revolutions, but magnified to a monstrous crudity — an aversion to culture, a hatred for civilization. Let no one be deceived: the urge toward the primitive is not a temptation that besets the Germans alone. The wish to fling off the burden and obligation of higher humanity is pushing to the surface among all masses.

This slave revolt of primitivism, this Calibanism, may appear in the pompous costume of Hercules. In reality the modern hero cult is nothing but weakness, incapacity, fear of effort, escape from the intellectual task of humanity. Weakness without this Hercules disguise is the second aspect of the new soul: it expresses itself as security at any price, a craving for security owing to increased fear of life. Everything may be surrendered, all one's humanity betrayed — anything for security. To pledge oneself to anybody who will guarantee it is part of a spiritual condition by no means restricted to the masses. This is what levels off all the distinctions of civilization, and puts the well-to-do citizen, the scholar, the clergyman, the officer, the nobleman, and the civil servant all on an equal footing with the great mass of the harassed, disinherited petty bourgeoisie and the laborers; it blows away hereditary views and principles like chaff, until men fall down before the evangelist of security. What irony that the miraculous prophets of safety promptly become prophets of living dangerously, and lead a security-loving clientele among the cruel hazards of bombed cities!

A century ago far-sighted men of all nations prophesied the rise of inorganic masses, and thus the climax of a crisis involving the destruction of all organic orders and structures. In France it was de Tocqueville, in Switzerland Jacob Burckhardt who foresaw this. In von Radowitz, the friend of King Frederick William IV, Prussia had a far-seeing herald of the mass age.

What does this phenomenon mean? Not the emancipation of

a Fourth or Fifth Estate, not the proletarian revolution that led to Communism and thus to a new, classless order of society; we have something that cannot bring new values to the world, but desires only to exploit some of the existing ones for itself, and throw overboard the others as mere ballast. Communism, in so far as it hopes to establish a new social order and a new economic structure, in so far as it represents enlightenment and rationalism, atheism and anti-Christianity, in so far as it is planned economy, socialism, and upholds the state as an end in itself, — in so far as Communism does all this, it remains short of the mass revolt, and is the last expression and refinement of the ideas that rose with the bourgeoisie; or else it has already reached the point of defending itself against the revolt of the masses. Communism is not itself this revolt. It is not the masses that rule in Soviet Russia, but a rather different type of new bourgeois and civil servant. Yet behind the Bolshevik order as well as the democratic, behind every social and state order of the present age, there lurks the real revolution, the anarchy of the masses. It means the destruction and leveling off of all values, the irreparable lowering of the general level, the destruction of orders and hierarchies; it is the victory of primitivism and imbecilism over every species of mind, form and creation. It lies behind all our strivings. This is reality: this is no political fiction, no condition deliberately induced by parties and regimes. It seems to be the inevitable destiny of the present age, and apparently today, as de Tocqueville predicted, there is no more question of preventing it at all, but only of guiding it in order to let it destroy as little as possible.

This is the question, far beyond any momentary political worries, that concerns our actual fate. There is no nation for which it does not represent destiny.

Hitherto perhaps most attention has been paid to the psychological condition of the masses, their particular kind of excitability, of lethargy, of susceptibility to temptation. But the shifts in the substance of the masses are no less significant.

The masses cease to be national. They are alike in all nations, and they react alike. They are a nationless element. National policy or national defenses can no longer be based on them. They are amorphous; they defy all molding. The masses cease to be a class. This is what the Left in politics does not realize. The masses cannot sustain civilization; they only consume the heritage of civilization; the masses are culture-blind. There have always been masses. The distinction between the present situation and the past is that all the orders of being dissolve into disembodied masses, while the whole trend of civilization points toward a universal mass condition. The modern masses are no longer a sinking, disintegrated element in the order of a social structure above them; they have become the one form in which society exists, the dominant form.

The third and greatest transforming force is the technological revolution. It too raises the question whether our fate as a technological age was not inevitable. Can there be in store for us any but one course — to fulfil the technological nature of our civilization and our humanity cleanly and without compromise, without romantic and traditionalist retrospects, without sentiment or resentments? If we are going to plan, and beget a new type of man, must we not be radical to the limit, and discard all tradition? Must we not simply draw the ultimate conclusion from our situation, and make man the servant of his creation, technology?

What is technology? Is it a means of human welfare, or is it not also the most effective instrument of human power concentration? Is not the meaning of technology domination and subjugation instead of the promotion of human comfort and enjoyment, as the bourgeois disciple of progress believes? If technology assumes the role of religion, it changes from an instrument of human welfare into an end in itself, and with that its innermost meaning, to wit the effective multiplication of power, establishes itself as a new political force. The concepts of technology are above all rational, efficient; they are bound to take as their aim the "organic construction of the world," "the efficient management" of life in its entirety. For this a new, concentrated and centralized exploitation of all technical resources is necessary. So technology gives rise to a new world, that of consistent, total efficiency.

Thus the changed world seems to indicate for itself the only lines along which it can be "given form." In this world of technology there are no qualities, only functions. In place of historic development we have efficient construction, in place of political conviction an assigned quota of work. At the center of this technological world is a general planning headquarters whose authority is beyond recourse. This is the ultimate phase of an intellectual movement that began with the dawn of enlightenment and rationalism. It means the reordering of the human world as a system of exact relationships.

Have the forms of our previous political and social life been able to withstand this shift of reality? Ought we not instead to find new ones, to conceive new regulative ideas? In any case this revolution in realities has limited the usefulness of our old standards of judgment. Enmities have become irrelevant; new alliances and new oppositions have grown up. Error and self-delusion have been the necessary accompaniment of such transformations. What might have been helpful is pushed aside, and what belongs in the enemy's arsenal is grasped at. The distinguishing mark of such a crisis is that everyone fights on the wrong front, perhaps combating the very thing he hopes to bring about, and accomplishing what he means to prevent. In such times there are no fixed alignments.

Does this mean that the great ideas and principles of Western European life have outlived their usefulness, and should be discarded? Or ought we not to seek refuge in these very principles, and put down the rising revolution?

No historical process can be reversed. The old has not outlived its usefulness, and neither can the new be completely eliminated.

The technological revolution, the rise of the masses and the deflation of all Western European standards cannot be undone. We must go beyond them; we cannot go back of them. History is an irreversible process. Anyone who tries to go back is certain to destroy the very thing he wants to achieve. But there is a third road, which does not lead to radical revolution, nor does it strive toward the past. This is the path by which the genuine forces of the new reality are accepted and joined in a new entity with lasting principles of the historical past.

THE ROAD TO BARBARISM

We are waiting, but for what? There is a sort of shudder, an apprehension in the air. Today's tranquility is charged with tension. It is a warm autumn day; I am standing in the quiet, remote sunken garden of Kensington Gardens, with its endlessly new blossoms. You see treetops beyond the arbored walk, and you are far away from all cities and all wars. There is a shifting sky of thunder-clouds and sharply outlined storm-clouds; spots of sunlight and shadow chase each other. A few yards from my feet, where I have been writing under the trees this summer, lies a time-bomb; beyond it yawns a great bomb crater, and then another a few yards from the tea-house. Severed branches and a scrap of a barrage balloon are dangling in a tree. I am snatching a brief rest in the sun while the world holds its breath; the beast from the deep is lurking in ambush.

The traces of devastation are increasing, but outwardly life has hardly changed. In spite of warnings the streets are crowded; no one heeds the air-raids. Streets are closed off here and there, and occasionally time-bombs explode, but the shops go on with their business, and the people show no fatigue. A tour on foot reveals scenes both touching and staggering. The family pictures still adorn the mantle on the upper floor of a vanished house, and souvenirs hang on the wall; fragments of rooms and furniture dangle into the abyss and out into the sunlight.

Nothing is gratis; man must pay the full price for his historical transformations. It is idle to surmise, as we did today, whether these ghastly events could have been avoided. Perhaps they could have — certainly in this form. But where were not only the leading men but the political groups far-sighted and influential enough to do what was necessary at the right time?

Is the combination of the new with the old life that we are still living, the new European entity, are the now inevitable new social and economic structures possible to conceive of without this intervention of ruthless force? How can we bring into being the new world center that is now irresistibly growing up, the great union of British and American states? There will be a new Mediterranean between Great Britain and America — the Atlantic basin, around which the coming great peaceable empire will arise, the Pax Atlantica.

The question of what Hitler will do, whether he will attack, whether he will not, fades beside this all-important question: will our strength be sufficient to bring us back from the war with a "glorious order" in the sense that this time we will do what is necessary before it is too late? Not simply new houses, a longer week-end, the abolition of social privilege, punishment of the guilty: not simply satisfaction of the most pressing needs, the sorest hunger: but a true great peace.

As yet this is all ahead of us on the far shore, at the end of our *Mayflower's* voyage. We have as a reality here barbarous devastation such as possessed and maniac men have never exceeded.

But we mistake its gravity if we see behind it merely the revolting face of a man with an odd lock of hair, and his accomplices. Nor did mere eternal Teutonic destructiveness give birth to this barbarism. The headquarters that today are ordering young German aviators to fire on women and children are only the signalmen on the barbarous railway; they did not invent barbarism. It sprouted from the very heart of our civilization long before these people were born.

It rose with the revolt of the masses, with their new animal character, beyond good and evil. It arose with the ideological unmasking of all human ideas and values during the process, once so glorious, of intellectual emancipation and human progress. It grew on the testing grounds of technology and in the precision work of applied science. This barbarism is the inevitable result of our changed reality. It is the naked countenance of the great revolution, a revolution that is not merely a metaphor but reality itself.

We must recognize the existence of this revolution, and distinguish its outward signs from its true substance. In this tortured city, amongst these heroically patient people, it is difficult to preserve calm enough to seek the deeper causes and relationships.

3

The Unseen Revolution

THE PRACTICAL POLITICIAN or statesman is in the habit of seizing on the most immediate motives and explanations. Remoter perspectives, deeper-lying causes seduce one to a long view that makes for short-sightedness in dealing with the important tasks of the day. But even a balanced judgment is endangered by the temptation to see things as simpler than they really are.

It would be over-simplifying and minimizing the character of our revolution to see it fundamentally as nothing but the man Hitler's attack on world peace, possibly with some features of a general economic crisis. Here there is a singular resemblance to people's obtusity about the French Revolution and its technique a hundred and fifty years ago. During those memorable twenty-five years of British opposition to the French Revolution, a larger understanding gradually made headway; it finally led to Castlereagh's accepting one of the most fundamental revolutionary principles. For instance he recognized that the war against Napoleon was no longer a cabinet-minister's war, but true national war. At that time the idea of a national war was as suspect to the accredited statesman as the idea of a world revolution is today.

If this example be applied to the present, we might expect the leading statesmen of this country to realize that what we have now is not a war of two empires for leadership in Europe, or self-defense by one power against the belligerence of another, but a universal civil war cutting across all nations and continents.

Moral indignation at the revolution is quite as futile as ignoring it. It constitutes an invasion of our civilized world by irrational forces, and thus necessarily is barbaric and destructive. It is the consequence of a development that was bound to go on to its final conclusion. Anti-humanism, barbarism, is implicit in the very machines that are the instruments of human progress. Progress and barbarism are more closely knit than Sigmund Freud supposed. There is a necessary connection between the two.

The naive view sees technology only as the triumph of the human will and reason over nature. It does not perceive the change in man himself, his own subjugation to the force of technology. The machine is what has transformed consciousness. It has created new spiritual automatisms; it is the source of a profound emotional devastation. It is then, with the spirit weakened and irritable, that the popular deflation of all ideologies and ethical values removes the necessary checks of the spiritual process, and puts man at the mercy of his reactions, under the stimulus of chance irritations and impulses. Thus we have fertile soil for a special misuse of the irrational social forces, euphemistically called propaganda.

The new masses grew up between the forces of a transformation recreating man from without and a transformation from within. Only economic crisis and political uncertainties were required to shatter the whole fiction of private security, leaving the masses helplessly to themselves and to their fear for existence.

In this upheaval the people ceases to be real. "The people is no longer a reality; there is nothing but masses," the cynical but acute Carl Schmitt, former Attorney General of the National Socialists, used to say. The articulated nation becomes a mere romantic memory. A policy based on the existence of such a nation is doomed to miscarry.

Was this not the case of France?

THE TRAGEDY OF FRANCE

The magical serenity of a Couperin drama shines through the smoky lounge of the hotel. The French broadcasts of the de Gaulle group are probably the best things yet done in the way of radio publicity. Consistency, variety in the programme, ingenuity and a high intellectual level give these broadcasts their effectiveness, without succumbing to popular superficiality. The whole wealth and clarity of the French mind, *esprit,* and wit shine forth from every broadcast.

But what about this "resistance to oppression," these great ideas of liberty, equality, human dignity and humanitarian progress, to which the broadcasts refer as to their inner soul? Certainly freedom lives, and will never vanish from the blood-stream of human history. What folly to try to "repeal" the French Revolution! How preposterous to abolish the universal rights of man politically, or throw them on the scrap-heap! If this were the intention of the new French government, everything would remain a farce. But is it actually that?

Allegiance to general ideas is cheap; but to give them institutional support now is the real task.

It was after Munich that I found myself one day talking with a number of highly intelligent Frenchmen, devout Catholics, high judges — one of them took me to Cardinal Verdier — about the inevitable military conflict with National Socialism. These men were profoundly dismayed by the prospect. They did not condemn Munich quite so sharply as Bernanos, who called the agreement "A macabre farce, a sort of miscarriage suffered by a France violated by hooligans while asleep in the woods." But they too spoke despairingly of France's inevitable downfall. To me it was like a reflection of what we felt in Germany during the years before the upheaval: the necessity to overcome lethargy and a wrong political order. It was enough to give one pause when people in almost all the Continental nations recognized the same necessity for a new integration of the people, a "réconciliation et réintégration du peuple sous les signes et dans l'esprit de l'ancienne France," as Bernanos put it for France.

We are depriving ourselves of a means for really comprehending our fate if we do not see the tragedy of France in its full scale. It was not only intrigues, not only a corrupt class, not an outrage perpetrated by ambitious cliques or senile reactionaries, that led to this desperate and tragically wrong notion of making terms with National Socialism. The full truth is that every level of the French people went on strike. They did not want to fight; they were tired of fighting, for once and for all. They wanted to live, even without honor if necessary, in the hope that they could still remain themselves. Is this the withdrawal from history, the relapse into the prophesied peonage that Hitler foresaw long years before the collapse? A nation that loses its belief in greatness, that sagely restricts itself to what is possible, remaining completely skeptical of great feelings and sacrifices, and contenting itself with intelligent enjoyment of the material good things of life, ceases to be a power in the making of history. The surrender of great political aims and a retreat to the mere defense of one's own property — as French policy was formulated after Munich — means the beginning of a logical trend toward a frugal resignation by which France believes she can continue to live in her immortal intellect even without the millions of French colonials, or actually as an occupied country.

A nation thus resigned obeys other laws than the glory of liberty, equality or *la patrie*. Is this not an effect of the changed consciousness I have just been discussing — the disappearance of whole series of concepts, the vanishing of the nationalist idea, of the social obligation inherent in the revolt of the masses? Masses that would no longer fight and make sacrifices because they were too sage and skeptical to believe in the reality of great words and values, a political elite too much concerned with the strategy of domestic politics to do what was necessary: this was France before the catastrophe — a mere stage set, a hermit crab nesting in the shell of another creature as if in too large a suit of armor, and knowing no better use for the historical traditions and obligations of the Grande Nation than to make pretty speeches about them.

III

The catastrophe came not merely because the nation was shattered, not merely because France "could watch no more tears being shed," not merely as a result of the universal hedonism; no, it was evident that the substance of the nation had evaporated.

Before the collapse, as today, the Catholic generals formed a mere false front for a no longer extant France. But the answer to the question why they did not sooner intervene shows the tragic bewilderment that had seized the nation. If they really had intervened, the very thing Hitler had been aiming at with his political war would have happened, namely the cleavage of the nation. There would have been plenty of strength for a political revolt to resist necessary reforms. There would have been political disturbances, but no great national upsurge. For this the pre-war period was not yet ripe. Consequently the Blum experiment too was bound to miscarry. There is nothing to do but to wait and hope for a miracle, and go on working in silence, as many of the more far-sighted statesmen had wished to do.

The real causes of these tragic events show the Second World War in its true light as a civil war. I see the same influences that drove German patriots into the arms of the Nazis. It is the identical, despairing determination to snatch from the error of its ways a self-deluded nation reeling onward in false security, in order to bring it to a rebirth out of the elements of its history and traditions. It is the same despairing determination and the same tragic bewilderment, ending in unfreedom and self-annihilation.

A French newspaper writes, very much as we before the upheaval used to dream of a new order: "The state will relieve itself of numerous tasks for which it is not competent." Or, further, it says that "the cells of France, the families, professions, regions," will "achieve the blessing of extensive decentralization." An official speech on the true condition of France says, "It was a politically, economically and socially exhausted State." Let us take from one statement a few outlines exactly corresponding to our judgment of the Weimar Republic ten years before: A "total reshaping" was necessary; it had been prepared for "through twenty years of uncertainty, discontent and covert resistance." Further, "For a long time a number of Frenchmen, particularly the younger generation outside the parties, which they found disgusting, had been voluntarily eschewing the corruption of public life, and dreaming of a political and moral regeneration for their native land." It is said of the future of Europe, "that great mistakes must be atoned for. Economic life depends upon cooperation within the order; this cooperation, free of all ideology, will replace the exclusively political forms of the European balance of power."

The sense of being at the end of an era was very lively before the war in circles of the French intelligentsia whose judgment on other matters differed widely. The Catholic elements saw this end as connected with the final phase of the great secularization that wound up in the French revolution. A quite unpolitical civil servant told me in 1938 that there was only one road back — a complete reeducation of the French nation from the ground up, abandoning intellectualism and the *École normalienne*. This alone might help prevent the crash. Pascal and Descartes were needed instead of Voltaire, Rousseau and the Encyclopedists. The seventeenth, not the eighteenth century must set the pattern. The

113

purport of several political conversations that I had during the disastrous winter of 1938–39 can be summed up as the anxiety of a class of desperate patriots, who had remained in the background, lest a France whose masses were so spineless and enervated, so reluctant to work and so unwilling to make sacrifices, should now be incapable of any heroic resistance. An effort must be made at all costs — even temporary humiliation — to gain time in which to train up a new France and preserve it from physical and intellectual death. For, these men argued, even biologically the nation was no longer able to afford great loss of blood. The abandonment of the land and the decline of the birth-rate must be stopped before the nation could afford to reckon with the losses of a great new war.

I do not think it is just or politically astute to condemn men who saw France's misfortune coming and tried to gain time by evading it, nor to class them with political desperadoes who played the parasite and tried to crowd into the limelight on every occasion. The tragic confusion lies in the fact that measures which might have meant regeneration before the collapse were impossible owing to unfavorable pre-war conditions; used in the desperation of defeat they can only conceal, or at least distract the nation's attention from, the full measure of its misfortune. In this way and through connections with destructive political elements and the victoriously occupying enemy, irreplaceable positive forces of real reconstruction have been discredited for the future. This is one of the greatest confusions of an age abounding in self-delusion and error.

THE POWERS OF REACTION

Those who consider themselves the powers of progress are in reality powers of reaction. Here is the paradox in the present crisis. We cannot get away from this relationship between progress and modern barbarism. Not only is it true of our outward and political life, but in our intellectual crisis too we are reversing a long process of human development. Belief in a single, moral god was the sustaining force of lonely great men tens of centuries before the Christian era. With this belief they confronted the masses, who deified the daemonic forces of nature, which they hoped to influence by magical rites. Far into the shadowy background of our human history this one series of spiritual giants has been the sole influence to which humanity owes its ascent; men impregnated with the force of their spirit have given up the altars of Baal, the sacrifices on the hilltops, and have served God in spirit and in truth.

This shining fire is opposed by another blaze. It is the vocation and the purpose of the great leading minds in our present late-Western Europe to get rid of belief in an intellectual and moral center; they celebrate their emancipation as an intellectual achievement. These new prophets of the god of national solidarity, of race, of mating, of the procreative force in nature, march forth wearing the halo of destruction to meet the God who is spirit. Our Western world is snatched back across the centuries into the old struggle of Israel against the idols, against the brazen calf of Baal, which today is called biology, and against Moloch, who is still the god of power and blesses his devotees with dominion gained through blood sacrifice. Humanity is in the desert again, trembling at the terrors and apprehensions of life; once more it resorts to magic rites, and bows down to men of violence who delude it with security.

Why is it that we remote descendants see intellectual greatness in such a process of devastation rather than in the law-givers of a higher humanity who, like the "man Moses," fight the beliefs of magic and fear with glad tidings of the one God who is not pleased by burnt offerings? It takes a long process of retrogression to make a person see spiritual greatness in destruction. Perhaps we needed these modern wizards and shamans to show us the desert we had strayed into.

We are shocked today at the utter abjectness of the mind, the venality of science, the byzantinism of scholars and artists. In reality this was all long since prepared for, indeed already existed — this new sophistry, this ability to justify anything and to serve anyone who would pay. Since long before the socialists came into power, the mind had ceased to take itself seriously. Behind the pretension of the scientific industry and loud emotional talk about beliefs there lay hidden a complete cynicism that mocked itself, and was ready to be the slave of any power whatever.

But it is no sign of strength to cast off the obligations of a greater humanity with the gesture of an emancipated superman, and then either to enjoy earthly pleasures or to surrender oneself without regret to the instincts of a blond beast, a brown one, or whatever the color may be. What all this resounding pseudo-heroism shows is not strength but weakness, sickness and inner slackening. It is reluctance to attempt the impossible — civilization; it is "dislike of civilization"; it is inertia, the sloth that even the medieval church counted among the deadly sins.

It has long been the task of the literati, who fancied themselves as the intellectual stewards of progress, to manufacture out of barbarism a counterfeit advance. Liberal enlightenment, which sees in religion nothing but an illusion, a morass of fear, apprehension, and primitive emotions, to drain which is the chief end of education for the human race, agrees with Freud — awful thought! — that the great majority of mortals are incapable of rising above the childishness of a religious outlook on life.

How close this intellectual progress comes to the source of modern barbarism, we can see in the conclusions which so great a leader of thought as Freud drew from the fact that life is harsh. We cannot live without palliatives, he says, and cites three: the distraction of interest, which makes us think little of our misery; substitute satisfactions; and intoxicants.

Here we are already at the heart of all such regimes as National Socialism, which use the susceptibility and psychic weakness of the uprooted masses as means to subjugate them politically by diversion, substitute satisfactions and intoxicants.

It is enlightenment, intellectual progress, that has furnished the weapons of spiritual seduction to the modern tyrannies. Misuse of progress is what leads to barbarism. But is "progress" itself not an abuse? Does not liberalism advance to its own destruction by following its own principles to their logical conclusions? This paradox takes us into a new quarter of the political maze. The proud assault on nature, the subjugation of natural forces to the human will, the subordination of life to the mastery of science

— this goal of enlightenment and progress did not result in an order whence, as we had hoped, pain was banished and where pleasure was the dominant principle. On the contrary, the humanitarian road leads straight back to bestiality. Enlightenment today is returning to the darkness whence it came. When every one of us moderns behaves to some extent like a paranoiac putting a wish-dream in place of a conception of the world that he cannot endure; when the humanitarian religions have to be regarded as a diversion for the masses — then we have attained complete nihilism, a chaos whence we can emerge only through the coercive order of a new absolutism, a modern tyranny.

Who shall deny that enlightenment has put its ineffaceable mark on humanity? Man as a reasonable being, man as an entity, were the ideas that made possible a general human norm, independent of origin and social position. Thus those ideas established clear standards of justice and injustice, good and evil, right and wrong as determined by reason. But today reason itself has been rendered questionable by enlightenment. The growth of ethnographic knowledge has unsettled the universal validity of human reason. This intellectual movement, this emancipation will remain one of the great lines in the development of the human race, which we cannot wish had never been, even though it did lead to the present state of utter turmoil. It is senseless to attempt the reversal of the process, as some men in Germany and France wanted to do. We must rather find the limits within which enlightenment and rationalism are beneficial. Not enlightenment itself must be combated, but its abuse by a reason grown autonomous, cast upon its own resources, and thus vulnerable to the first outside attack.

We were still touched by the whole splendor of humanism just before the nightfall of modern barbarism. In our younger days we took part in the rise of a free humanity with all the riches of an inexhaustible heritage. Later, when we began to reflect after the intellectual sack of Rome, the words of a humanism warmed by youthful enthusiasm were what urged us on, because this enthusiasm made people feel able to snatch the world from barbarism. But could they? Did they not succumb to the very weakness shown in the capitulation of the mind? Why was humanism powerless to resist all the inroads of rising nihilism? Why did its champions capitulate one after another, and make a treaty with progressive barbarism?

A noble and ennobling humanity is the very end and aim of humanism. But what part of man does humanism love? Man as he is? An ideal image?

What does this love of man aim at? Welfare and harmony. It wishes to reject evil; it refuses to recognize evil. What a strange view of mankind — what a suppression of reality! "Man is good," the phrase of Rousseau, the message of the French Revolution and of all enlightenment, is false. Man is not good. The optimistic image of mankind is what renders humanism weak. Man possesses both the creative force of a spirit striving from darkness into light, as Goethe put it, and the urge toward ruin, toward destruction and self-annihilation. No matter what modern interpretation we may choose to put upon this other side of humanity — dislike for civilization, the night side of culture — we may just as well stick to the old, Christian term, *evil*.

We learn to distinguish between an "adventist" humanism, the last flowering of pre-Christian antiquity, and an "apostate," self-sufficient humanism, which postulates man himself as the sole standard and meaning of life.

Does what is called the autonomous man exist? Is not this to deny the profoundest and most fruitful development of the human spirit, which has led from the Judaism of the prophets through ancient humanism to Christianity? Humanism without the Christian spirit is empty; humanism without Christian earnestness is irresponsible; humanism without the ethical backbone of Christianity is weak.

If we oppose humanism it is not for the reason that makes Pareto or National Socialism and Fascism condemn it — not because it is the sign of weakness, to which man succumbs only when he becomes decadent and his instinct grows uncertain; but because man on his own resources alone cannot overcome evil — the destructive element in his nature.

If we utter a word like "evil," if we accept it as a reality, the entire intelligentsia of both hemispheres at once suspect us of being narrow-minded reactionaries. But evil *is* a reality. It cannot be juggled away out of our lives. Humanism, relying on the goodness of man's nature, thus produces its own complement, cynicism, euphemistically called realism, which relies on the incorrigible animality of the mammal, Man. Instead of a universal pattern that unites all human beings, we have a clash destroying all order, because one interpretation of life remains an intellectual luxury, an oratorical flourish, while the other dominates actual conditions. Humanism opens the door for the supremacy of cynicism, and cynicism furnishes the plausible motives for capitulation to force, for adaptation to actual circumstances, which always denotes a flight toward security.

Humanism is no salvation from the general peril of mankind. Hence there is but one remaining escape: submission to a visible and authoritative force. Such a force alone can give security now that an invisible, intellectual authority is no longer to be believed in. Except for this flight toward security there is nothing but a flight into adventure, into the sedative of activity. This is escape forward, the aggressive onward push to overcome fear in the excitement of action.

The true forces of reaction are not to be found where, politically, they are usually sought — in the cliques of a privileged class, among purblind reactionaries who want to order life back into older and outworn forms, in the eternally human desire to enjoy privileges and benefit by social discrimination. This form of reaction, of class consciousness, is innocent by comparison with the forces of reaction that would crowd higher human life back to primitivity, irresponsibility, bestiality.

THE DOUBLE FACE OF SOCIALISM

Furlough, peace, sound sleep, fresh air. Here in the country you really begin at last to notice the pressure of the weeks behind, the accumulated fatigue. There is a nipping coolness out here. As guests at this old and venerable country seat we are engulfed by the atmosphere of a great past; in the park with the busts of old

Romans along the garden wall, with the swans on the plant-grown brook, in the stillness of this serene old village, the war vanishes; the beast crawls away behind the hedge. A great world, a spiritual world with all the riches of a mature life, opens its blossoms again.

At night we go out on the terrace. The horizon flickers and flares; distant roaring and rumblings. Yonder lies the front, the great metropolis — the front — just as it was in the last war, only this time the city itself is the front.

But the beast comes over even here: through the hush of the night passes the drone of planes above. Even so, how you do sleep in these marvelous beds, with an embroidered canopy overhead, and old pictures on the walls! The mysterious voice of old houses speaks in its deep tones at night; you can feel yourself joining the orbit of a great tradition.

It is the moderation, the restraint, the wise avoidance of extremes, that gives this British life its elasticity. After the thoughts of the past few weeks upon the paradoxical union of progress and barbarism, the question of how to escape from the vicious circle finds an answer here.

It is not compromise alone that has kept political life healthy here. The reason why people in this country have remained capable of true compromise lies in their instinctive delimitation of life, in people's reluctance to think their thoughts through to the bitter end. It is no more consonant with human limitations to pursue principles and trains of thought to their conclusion than it is to be absolutely right as an individual. This is the explanation of how British life has remained sound in the present spiritual crisis. It is virtually free of doctrines and theories. Only when these irreplaceable elements of Western European life are pursued to their extreme, where they are altogether reversed, does the emancipation of liberalism become self-destruction, and socialism not a great achievement in equitable agreement, but tyranny. If we carry our regulative ideas through to their logical conclusion, if we posit them absolutely, they become nonsense, and destructive of life. Any idea becomes absolute when it is exaggerated into a doctrine, when we make a system out of it and proclaim it as a right or a goal to be absolutely and uncompromisingly striven for, when it professes to be more than an adjunct to experience and an instrument of an ever-changing order. There lie the roots of our disastrous German destiny. It is this mania for following everything to its ultimate conclusion and making a system out of it that has brought us again and again to spiritual and political catastrophe.

Scarcely anything could be better calculated to give one confidence in England's future than the fact that here even socialism is not doctrinaire, but instead, being free of Marxism, is a practical, open-minded, social reform party.

Does doctrinaire Marxism as a force of practical policy belong to the past? This would mean finding not merely a new language for the socialist party and the workers' mouthpieces that have hitherto spoken in Marxian accents, but new methods for the shaping of the political will. Hitler has thought it no shame to admit that he owes many of his methods and political insights to Marxism; and that he had the courage to carry out what political Marxism, in Germany at least, could only anticipate in intellectual blueprints, but had not dared to execute. This is a rather disagreeable and, incidentally, unjust statement, which the official representatives of German Marxism in exile resented my recording and publishing.

There is much in the present order of society that is antiquated, and much that should be swept away. But among the most antiquated rubbish of all is the Continental doctrinarianism born of rationalistic and unhistorical notions, and now beginning to establish itself even beyond the European continent. The world of the nineteenth century has died. Surely this means that the remnants of feudal orders, last strains of a Victorian and Wilhelmine age, should be cleared away. But this insubstantial belief in progress, the pseudo-humane optimism, the maniac rationalism and the cheap faith in mundane things all belong to the world of the nineteenth century. Hegel, just as much as Marx, belongs to the nineteenth century, national-democratic state individualism as much as Greater Prussian absolutism; but so too does the expectation of making man, by means of external institutions, into something other than what he is — a double being with all the everlasting inadequacy of him whose real vital element is duality.

Certainly National Socialism has absorbed and developed to their ultimate radical conclusions all the nationalist and militarist impulses that our so-called reactionary nationalism had been making political capital of for decades. But that is not what makes it so dangerous, and it is not as a new form of Pan-Germanism or Prussian militarism that it has hitherto been irresistible. It has developed its immensely destructive political forces from the weakness of the various orders opposing it and from the exploitation of tools and methods developed and prepared, not in a nationalist, but in a socialist Marxist medium. These tools are undoubtedly calculated to destroy on a monstrous scale, but never to build a new world.

Here is the task that seems not to be understood. We must find a new order that will furnish institutional organs for our democratic form of life, the imperishable product of a rich historical development; yet we must not borrow these organs from the mortal enemy, totalitarian tyranny.

Does potential progress in a solid, reasonable sense lead toward an all-embracing rational order, a universal collective? Is this the goal of the future? Or is it not rather the very opposite, a living equilibrium of many independent forces, none of them capable of total domination? But does not this mean that all these absolutist doctrines and theories of salvation by materialism, historical or otherwise, and all ideas of efficient planning belong in one and the same camp? Confronting it, in the other camp, stands everyone who professes allegiance to freedom, democracy, a balance of forces, initiative, the moral responsibility of the individual, the preservation of privacy, intellectual and moral independence, the rise and advance of civilization and Western European culture. The resulting questions prove that middle class and workers must no longer combat each other; they are partners on the same front.

By nature German social democracy is dual. It is improper to reproach it with having been too democratic to seize or defend power illegally in the years before the great crisis. This very fact expressed one side of it: the feeling of responsibility and the truly democratic trait of restricting one's own desire for political power, and submitting to objective ideas of justice. We should therefore not attack the leading Social Democrats for steering a moderate course; instead we should be grateful that they made a new labor movement possible for the future, and preserved intact the moral basis on which that movement will achieve a special significance through leadership in the future peace.

But there is another face of the old Social Democracy. Here one root of modern totalitarianism grew. On this soil there run riot all the poisonous plants that in themselves have nothing to do with a labor movement and the aim of a just social order — atheism, consistent historical materialism, rationalism, emancipation of the flesh and the mind, and also all the concepts of total coercion. These are dictatorship, planning, leveling, collectivization to the point of compulsory faith, and a racial "science" based on selected premises. As if the science of our orthodox Marxists with its axiom of historical materialism were less strictly predicated upon its ends and had been less intentionally made dependent as an "ideological superstructure" upon definite social presumptions than the "race-conditioned" science of National Socialism! As if everything now grotesquely perverted into the irrational racism of National Socialism had not found its full-grown prototype in rationalist Marxism! Even the officially party-accredited athletic clubs, cultural leagues, literatures with their own party slang, the regulator troops, parades, flags and rites gave the example for the brown battalions and all the organizations of National Socialism.

This is the second face of Social Democracy, that indisputably great movement on behalf of the laboring population. Nobody can doubt the enormous amount of educational work and positive accomplishment due to the movement. If the German worker has been among the best and most dependable types in modern Germany, it is due solely to the tirelessly working generations of anonymous socialist teachers and leaders. But this precious work is paralyzed by the doctrine and practice of a collectivization that needs only another denominator in order to become what predominates today — the revolutionary movement of nihilism.

Consequently a decision is necessary. Which will the future labor movement fight for? For the latter aspect, an alien accretion to the true core of Social Democracy? Or for the former — the education of responsible personalities on the principles of Western European civilization? To cling further to both lines of development could not but paralyze the state- and history-making power of Social Democracy. It would then be not a factor of future accommodation and balance, but an inexhaustible hotbed of latent revolutionary disintegration. We must go beyond this duality, and decide in favor of the law under which this our continent began its historical life two thousand years ago.

A great labor movement can be the political and social keystone in Europe, the sustaining foundation of a permanent peace. But it will be impossible if socialism clings to the wish-dream of a radical new social order that can be realized only by some species of modern tyranny. If the question is how to harmonize the institution of property and private business with the new concentration of the means of production and the social functions, it will not be hard for true traditionalism to reach a lasting agreement with socialism.

Doctrinaire socialism, on the other hand, can never be made a reality without tyranny. Dictatorship, which according to socialist doctrines ought to be a mere educational transition, is bound to be permanent in a socialist society.

"There can be no practicable socialism except by authoritarian means," says Pirot. "In our era authority is exercised by the state within the structure of the nation." It will be objected that we must go beyond the national state to true internationality — that the state within the national structure is the very thing to be obviated. Certainly this is the ulterior idea of the most recent socialism, in so far as it has recognized the impossibility of putting its doctrine into effect on the level of national states. What would not work within the structure of the individual nation and the national state might be possible in a socialist Europe or in a true political universe.

The socialists are undoubtedly right to the extent that no new order can be created within the confines of the separate national states in either a social or an economic sense, nor even politically. One of the tasks that we must therefore set ourselves in the future is to obviate the state within the confines of the nation. But what takes its place? The super-state, the centralized aggregate State, the international State for social functions, with all its temptations of power and violence for an omnipotent elite?

4

The Assimilation of the Revolution

WE HAVE HEARD a new speech by Churchill, of classic cast and with all his masterly skill at saying in the simplest words, in sentences of ageless perfection, exactly what weighs unspoken and inarticulate on every man's mind. Is it going too far to detect a Shakespearean touch in the words that can inspire alike the man in the street and the most cultivated intellect?

This nation does not need mass hypnosis or stimulation to mass psychosis in order to withstand the supreme test. There is no better sign of the soundness of this life and of the fact that the process of mass leveling has found its limit here. In his speeches we can see something like a positive opposite pole to the thing called propaganda, which has a negative pole in the malevolent, disintegrative demagogy that tempts the masses. Such demagogy is in the deepest sense wasteful husbandry, destroying spiritual forces, and therefore bound sooner or later to bring savage retribution upon the nation that succumbs to it. These speeches of Churchill's show that despite the revolt of the masses there is a language which appeals with intuitive accuracy to a nation without intoxicating it, and without putting it in the hypnotic condition needed by the totalitarian shamans with their magic drums to make their masses believe. It is straightforward language, as against a speech panting, mad, and consumptive; it is a manly language as against the screeching of a wily female hysteric; it is the language of a good conscience as against a long-winded self-interpretation that conceals from itself but poorly the sense of coming disaster.

We feel certain that the future of the present century is being decided here. It is a moral decision. In this moral decision everyone shares, through the way in which he endures his destiny. The mosaic of a regeneration and transformation of life is composed of these many small elements. Delicate women achieving the incredible in help, courage and endurance; children singing amid the ruin and shock of a collapsing house; men in danger of their lives helping, rescuing, clearing up placidly and without haste. Homeless groups of the poor waiting with admirable patience in the streets of the city at the entrances to the underground shelters. Business men stoically carrying on their business — bombed out of office and shop a moment ago, now already picking up the broken threads and carrying on their work.

It takes many features drawn from one's personal knowledge to bring the picture to life. There is scarcely anyone now who has not been close to the threat of death, or had some providential escape. There are families that have been repeatedly bombed out of their homes; there are families that have lost their all. One hears many experiences of death and destruction, property ruined and hopes crushed. But above it all is the constellation of indomitable humor, of a strong heart replying to danger with a joke instead of a quaver or a curse.

If there is any spot in the world whence destiny can be mastered, this city, this country is it. Here a genuine possibility of vanquishing nihilism exists. For we cannot terminate the war and the revolution with a new League of Nations; instead we must lay the foundations of a higher order even during the present war. One cannot construct anything outside reality, cannot schematically anticipate reality. The development of a new order must take place concretely. Therefore it is indispensable for the new order to have an actual nucleus of power, a full reality in one place.

Do we recognize the fact of a universal revolution, the fact that behind the military and political aggression of the so-called young nations and the rise of the totalitarian regimes there are at work true revolutionary forces that the old regulative elements cannot simply ward off, but must assimilate? The future and the possibility of a great peace will depend on how well people understand the nature of the revolution, and whether they are willing to assimilate its productive elements.

Accordingly we must not simply ask what we are to consider definite and irrevocable in the external revolution already completed, i.e. what can be undone only with renewed loss and general detriment; we must ask also which of the revolutionary tendencies hitherto exploited by the totalitarian regimes accords with a changed reality, and therefore ought to be incorporated as a positive element in the historical tradition of Western Europe — what should be promoted as a sound force of true progress and regeneration, and what should be combated as a subversive tendency of revolutionary nihilism or doctrinaire utopianism.

Can we tell with any certainty at this early date?

The danger of the coming development lies in our mistaking inevitable social, economic and political reforms for doctrinaire utopianism, which demands a definite and permanent world order. If we oppose the idea of an efficiently planned order, we are suspected today of being reactionaries. Doctrinarians of all shades are even willing to accept general servitude and a lower standard of living for the masses as part of the bargain so long as their rational plan gets its due, whereas the natural and healthy process would be to introduce planning only where it and it alone can achieve the desired increase in economic security and social justice. Social reforms and the restriction or elimination of special privileges are necessary. But this merely requires a new condition of justice, not something new created from the rationalistic elements of a doctrine and the irrational elements of a social myth.

In the end there are but two ways out of chaos. We may draw all the conclusions from the technological revolution and the rise of the masses; this makes a rationalist, coercive order inevitable. Or else out of the great Western tradition, the historic forces that have hitherto determined the destiny of the European nations, we may form an order that will adapt itself to the new features of reality, but still represent a continuing development of previous tradition.

Is there any third, intermediate choice? Is there a social-revolutionary solution in addition to the radical and the traditionalist solutions?

132

The only answer to this is *no*. There is none. Any such solution would inevitably slip into the path of the radical-totalitarian solution, continuing along it to the same conclusion as previous coercive solutions. On the other hand the social or socialist features do certainly belong in the Western European tradition, and are destined to form the basis for its regeneration. But only on one condition: they must lay no claim to exclusiveness. This means a very great change; it is to be feared that even today political socialism is not ready to surrender its claim to exclusiveness in regulating the future, nor to take its place as simply one element in the Western European tradition. But the forces that call themselves traditionalistic are perhaps no less strong in their refusal. What we need is a new, larger conception of the Western European tradition.

In previous historical crises Great Britain has been distinguished by her capacity to assimilate revolutionary forces, thus avoiding state or social disasters. It has been the talent of Great Britain to divert the stream of revolution into the channel of evolution by reforms made in time. There is no question that this ability is closely connected with the unshaken endurance and vigor of the British Commonwealth. Apparently this gift of assimilating new forces in time has not been lost. *The Times* recognizes that there are elements in the National Socialist regime and its economic policies which take account of a new world situation, while the old orthodox views have now proved inadequate. The paper goes on to speak of the great changes in economic conditions. Such changes demand an adaptation, a correction of our existing views, which may be as drastic as the correction of our military views by tanks and planes. Obstinacy in clinging to methods and doctrines that were sound fifty years ago will be costly, it is remarked. *The Times* mentions economic and social changes, the assimilation of revolutionary measures for employment, for the creation of a British trade cooperative; investments must serve national ends, not merely private profit; retrenchments and sacrifices must be apportioned in accordance with social justice. In certain fields competition must be eliminated by monopolies. This sort of willingness to compromise is not capitulation to the difficulties of the war: because, as *The Times* says, the British democracy is capable of a new order based on mutual responsibility.

Churchill defines this in his cameo style as the reconciliation of democracy and tradition, which has succeeded in Great Britain. He too declares for a properly organized economic and social order, but founded on freedom of thought and speech, guarded by free elections and a free parliament. Here we have the will to make a synthesis of the new with that part of the old which must not be surrendered.

The congress of trades unions asserts that it is destined to rebuild the national life after the war. Social and economic institutions must give assurance that the elementary needs of every human being shall be satisfied. Food, clothing and shelter must be available to everyone.

This proves very clearly the determination to make necessary reforms, changes that will prevent a catastrophic breach with the existing elements of order. But it is no less necessary to realize that adequate reforms must not be confused with small installments paid to the new age. The longer the outward revolution lasts, and the more elements of the old political and economic order are eliminated, the more clearly we see the extent of the revolution, whose positive forces will have to be taken into the new order. The reforms include not only economic and social problems, but those of national policy and the state. Any attempt to render political problems nonexistent by economic means would be illusory, just as no new political order can replace a social order.

The reforms should not, on the other hand, include the typical means of creating a revolution, the implements of domination and the elements of mass manipulation. If we are to steer revolution into evolution, and assimilate the positive elements of the revolution, we must distinguish between these means of domination, these destructive tendencies, on the one hand, and the positive element in general on the other. Self-delusion and doctrinaire incorrigibility, beginning at this point, have led to the disastrous errors and mistakes of the present age.

Neither can there be the camouflaged smuggling-in of the revolution itself, which happened in Germany without our realizing it; nor must there be what I may call an induced abortion of the revolution. The latter was also attempted in Germany by the reactionary groups that did indeed see the true force of the revolution, but wanted to annihilate rather than assimilate it. Such an abortion consists in staging an artificial revolution, like the "national awakening" in Germany, in order to exhaust, divert or discipline the upsurging forces and then to finish the whole movement by an ultimate reactionary solution.

So far as the smuggling-in of the radical revolution through initial reform goes, this is the usual means by which the revolutionary elements work into key positions. They then undertake what the National Socialists called the second phase of the revolution, and what has been in other revolutions the typical process of radicalizing the leading elite. The danger still exists that the revolution kept from the front door by prompt reforms may get through a back door into the kitchen, and thence into the parlor. The demands of the revolutionists are not so dangerous as the methods taken to achieve them. And here, it must be admitted, there is a threat even to the politically healthy life of the Anglo-Saxon democracies. The absolutely vital question is whether the spokesmen of the revolutionary forces persist in claiming exclusive authority for their views and demands, or whether they are ready to recognize the rights of the others, the minority, the opposition. That is, are they willing to respect the vital law of democracy, compromise and negotiation? The decisive point will be whether they cling to the outworn conception of a social overturn and the utopian image of an ideal society.

In the field of foreign affairs no return to the system of small, completely sovereign nations is possible. Nationalism will always be an element of European life, but it no longer fits into state patterns. Not only business but the legal forms of social existence demand a larger area. The question is to find these forms, and with them the forms of inner order. This is one of the tasks of preparing for peace, but it must not consist of the drawing of frontiers and the creation of new nationalist democratic states with new peace treaties.

National Socialism today is building something like a basis for a Europe where nationalism no longer exclusively determines social life. In that way it gives effect to a genuine force of revolutionary regeneration. It sets the themes of the future order, but does not furnish the solution. The great European and universal order will grow up through free cooperation, not through the methods of coercion and domination. This is why Great Britain is destined for leadership, because she alone in the world has developed, for the greatest of all empires, a method of leadership instead of domination. She has, as Churchill says, united empire and liberty.

To a certain degree National Socialism has performed the historical function of liquidating an old situation. Even more its function is to reduce a number of doctrines to absurdity. It would be dangerous to regard the removal of old regulative elements and the elimination of a social structure as the sole lasting result of this tremendous experiment. Beyond question some circles think this or something like it is the significance of National Socialism in the march of history. In my opinion the historical function of National Socialism, at least in Germany, is to free Western European civilization from the deformation produced in the course of intellectual and technological revolution. It does so by showing whither this unrelenting progress, this technification and mass leveling, this social upheaval, this utopian idea of planning, and also this nationalist aspiration and these imperialist intentions with their political concomitants and their intellectual and moral consequences, are bound to lead. The function of National Socialism is to show the Western world the reverse of the picture. It thus necessarily restores to all thinking people the courage for self-assertion, for preserving their own nature.

THE NEW ABSOLUTISM

Anyone who remains conscious of the background to our historical development while living in the present age is bound to be struck by its similarity to the problems and solutions of the seventeenth century even more than by its resemblance to the Napoleonic wars and the struggle over the meaning and limitation of the French Revolution. There is going on today a struggle for absolute power — against the last great autonomous forces, against indirect powers, against all "particularity" — similar to the struggle in the age of baroque.

Unexampled confusion reigns in that struggle. In the foreground, under cover of the most varied disguises and self-delusions, there is an embittered combat to see who shall possess the new sovereign power — who is to lay hands on absolute authority. This is the struggle for the substance of the new absolutism: shall it be political forces from the old Left or the old Right that are to provide the dominant and, in future, irremovable elite? But whether the elite comes from left or right will make little difference in the character of the new absolutism, which follows its own natural laws. The pretenders to the throne all agree that absolutism itself is inevitable and necessary.

In the background another battle goes on — the effort to find an escape from these forced alternatives, and an escape from the blind alley that ends in absolutism. It is a fight against the new absolutism itself. This fight is being carried on by insufficient forces, and only half understood. Reactionary groups confuse their desire to be themselves the sovereigns of the new absolutism with the fight against the new tyranny itself. Liberal groups, who are for democratic liberty, justice, and a humanitarian order, cannot see that in their practical policy they are furthering the tendencies of a leftist absolutism. Socialist groups, in turn, believe they cannot enforce their desire for a new and juster social order except by political and economic planning that cannot function unless, actually, it becomes the new absolutism. There are also Christian ecclesiastical groups who wish to re-establish the arrangement (important and salutary in its day) of a worldly order of salvation through the Christian ethic, and who in its pursuit are bound to have recourse to a machinery that would be nothing but another form of absolutism. And then there is the gaudy palette of the romantics of all sorts, who hope to realize the old Holy Roman Empire or some other utopia.

But is not the very fight against the new absolutism utopian? There is no denying that what always happens in the field of practical politics keeps tending in that direction. This development parallels the relentless technification of our life. The state itself is a technological machine, and the ordering of society too requires machines that act to perform rational functions. At the same time this development is the reaction to the phenomenon of the modern masses. One might say that the new absolutism is not an arbitrary invention of ambitious potentates, any more than it was in the seventeenth century, but the necessary consequence of autonomous forces in decay. The new absolute power develops by including the vacant spaces left by the extinction of old, organic regulative forces.

Although rationally it seems so obvious that the future belongs to the technological machine functioning with absolute precision, even in the field of social and state life, this cannot be what definitely renders the new absolutism inevitable. Here, on the contrary, are the great tasks of our age. Without some limitation upon the effectiveness of the machinery and upon centralized absolutism, the whole struggle for democracy and personal liberty is mere toying with words. In that case the present great war is nothing more than a duel between two rival power groups; it is no longer a fight for freedom. Without it the British Empire, the liberties of a British commonwealth and of the United States, are but curious antiques that have survived through favoring circumstance in a changed world, like a medieval building amid modern factories.

But how can we counteract the destructive effects of technology and the rise of great mass collectives except by efficient machinery and an absolutist order? Where is the new institutional safeguard of liberty and individual responsibility in an age of collectives born of fear and craving for security? Security assured only by the new absolutist state, the new absolutist society, the new, total, universal collective?

Here is the great temptation of the present age — the ubiquitously lurking method of escape from present difficulties into a new absolutism that presents itself as the sole guarantee of at least outward order. Absolutism, and not totalitarianism. The connection of modern absolutism with that of the seventeenth century is no accident. Modern absolutism is the refrain and continuation of the seventeenth-century motifs. The decisive advance is not merely in the efficiency of the modern technological tools of power, which make any resistance utterly out of the question; it is above all in the necessary extension of the public domain to the mental sphere, to what we call personal faith, beliefs, private life.

It is essential to recognize that future law-givers cannot freely decide between destroying and preserving the elements that make up a private inner world, intellectual and conscientious liberty; the answer to this question is inherent in the nature of modern absolutism. The history of the nineteenth century showed that the old division into two spheres, within and without, which the monarchist absolutisms of the seventeenth and eighteenth centuries still rendered tolerable, is impossible today because with it the state or any absolute social order would be illusory. In the nineteenth century this division brought forth the liberal state, and out of this liberal state grew all the problems that engaged the nineteenth and the first half of the twentieth century, and rendered the state the football of interested groups and the new masses. Now the course of events is returning toward absolutism, having as it were described a circuit by way of guaranteeing a sphere free from absolutism. If absolutism becomes a reality today, if we must accept it, it can only be in the form of total absolutism, where there is neither an inner nor a private sphere, but only a tyranny determined by coercion, terrorism and collectivization in every aspect of life.

We meet the temptation of the new absolutism along many paths — by way of the necessity for a functioning state body; by way of an indispensable bureaucracy; by way of an intended universal economic management, of social planning. It is more than a mere joke that managed currency and concentration camps differ only in degree. Such state measures as consumption quotas and production schedules are possible only in a system determined to employ the most rigorous punishments if necessary to compel obedience. The ruling elite cannot freely choose the methods of regulation it deems desirable. Every system of public order has certain inevitable methods of attainment and maintenance that go with it. In a system of centralized total planning the resources of coercion cannot be dispensed with.

Nobody can deny that, whether tempted by absolutism or not, we must do today many things tending in that direction, because there is no other recourse. It is impossible above all to wage war, totally absorbing as it is, without elements of absolutist coercion. But even setting war aside, the economic crisis and the necessity of social reconstruction present problems that cannot conceivably be solved without the aid of special authorities and great centralized machinery, and that inherently and irresistibly tend toward consolidation in an all-embracing absolutist power machine.

The outward appearance of National Socialist doings must not distract us from recognizing that simple mass demagogy, a mere state of exaltation, is dominant in Germany, and that the irrational factor in life is glorified; but all practical undertakings are planned and conducted by rational methods. The reality in present-day Germany is a monstrous machine, a central mechanism. Though originally created in the shape of total war mobilization, its actual essence is that of a total planned economy — political, economic and social planning on rational lines and with an efficient force far exceeding anything done by the Soviet Union.

It is a mistake to regard as mere preparation for war the total mobilization of all the forces of society according to an inclusive plan. What really counts is not the purpose, but the actual mobilization of all latent forces, the coordination of all individual elements and the "straightening out" of every department of life according to a general plan. Take away the demagogic, hysterical part, and still you have the substance of a totally mechanized human world. What would distinguish it from political planning for the general good? Only the subjective fictions. The actual reality would be hard, objective, implacable, just the same.

The danger facing the whole civilized world today consists in the fact that we must mobilize all our forces in order to survive the present world crisis, and that the machinery for directing this mobilization becomes an end in itself, subjecting all life to its own control. All administrative machineries tend to become an end in themselves, let alone machines armed with the perfected power of absolutism.

None of these questions, which absorbed a small group of us in Germany ten years ago, have yet become irrelevant. It is only now that they are coming within the purview of the great Western democracies. For example, is not the competitive system so completely destroyed and discredited that it can be replaced only by universal planning, managed consumption and production outside the mechanism of the market? This is what people today call an economy of supplied demand, which means that the demand does not consist of the sum of millions of individual desires,

but is determined by plan according to noneconomic requirements. At that time we thought we could combine the advantages
of planned management with those of free competition. The actual fact was that the weaknesses of both economic systems pre-
dominated, and then gave way to the triumph of total planned
economy.

At that time we put our trust in the forces of self-government
and believed we could arrive at an order in which business and
the social functions would develop into corporate bodies in their
own right. We believed that we could extend this element of
autonomy to the institutions of intellectual life as well as the
specialized fields, and thus create a sort of plural state structure.
But was self-government possible at all in this age of mechanization? Is it not one of the most pronounced features of our new
reality that autonomous bodies in their own right merely obstruct
traffic? Today bureaucratization is regarded as the inevitable
consequence of our technological age. But the worst part of
bureaucracy is the elimination of personal responsibility. The
splendid results unquestionably obtained by applying the principles of mechanical efficiency to administrative work are thus paralyzed. The danger in every machine lies in the evasion of responsibility. The temptation exists because a machine performs
acts that the individual would never make himself responsible
for. The anonymous machine takes the responsibility for the most
unmoral actions. This taking refuge behind the machine is what
has allowed terrorism to spread in all the totalitarian countries.
Bureaucracy too, therefore, hardly offers a means of avoiding absolutism, any more than do economic and social planning.

THE ASSIMILATION OF THE REVOLUTION

ABANDONING THE BAGGAGE

Back to London, back to the world's heart. We find ourselves in a familiar atmosphere; one air-raid alarm has just ended, and a new one begins as we drive past the airport. We see fliers preparing to take off, and a plane lands. Past great new scenes of destruction; as I turn down my street I hold my breath; is our building still standing? Along the way through the familiar streets the rebuilding stands out amid the new devastation. Shops are open again, despite unglazed windows; there is no capitulation.

You can feel the tension again, feel yourself snatched back to this life of steel, into this tremendous destiny that lends importance even to the small; here is a new creation bleeding, battling, ever and anon marshaling its forces out of agony. We have lost any conception of security; we are but the prey of uncertainty, conscious of death from second to second. We are human beings on the brink of eternity once again, as in legendary ages, with ever-present death at our sides.

Leaf fires in Kensington Gardens; acrid, healthy smoke drifts among trees nearly bare now. Here and there you can still lie in a deck chair in the sun. At night, down again to the steerage, aboard the *Mayflower,* amongst the familiar faces; mankind is on the way, on the great trek, as Smuts says.

But on its way how is it to pass between Scylla and Charybdis, chaos and tyranny?

People on the march, with a long, painful road ahead of them, will yield to the temptation to abandon their baggage in their weariness. Drop everything, begin over again from the raw root

— this is a feeling that stalks anyone undergoing these trials. I think the weariness of civilization, the disgust with culture that so profoundly influence the new barbarism, should not be mistaken for the mere product of education by unscrupulous demagogues. It is not the doctrinarians alone who discard all their inherited baggage and spin their radical utopias like cobwebs over the abyss; the burden of civilization is growing too heavy for whole nations. They refuse to go on carrying the baggage of their history and their past.

Among the baggage is democracy. Some people want to be rid of it because it hampers them in their "fresh start," others because it provides no sufficient protection against the rising chaos. On both sides there are those who openly admit their aversion to democracy and those who think it sound pedagogy to preserve at least a fiction of democracy.

At bottom most of the champions of democracy, in so far as they had to do with the political realities, and did not simply argue or write articles, no longer were at all sure it was possible to preserve the sublime and fragile forms of democratic life intact against the assault of the masses and the new radicalism. Therefore they looked for what they could borrow from their adversaries' political thinking and methods. Deep down in their hearts they themselves wished desperately to throw off as impediments all the embarrassments of democracy, so that they could give prompt and objective attention to urgent matters, unhampered by the weight of domestic politics.

It has become popular to appropriate the political teachings of a cynical realism. All the more necessary for us to acknowledge emphatically that this is not how matters stand. The democratic form of our political and social life must not be surrendered. It is identical with the nature of our civilization.

There are two possibilities. Either you may try to develop, from the principles of historical democracy, new forms of political leadership and control and new forms of institutional safeguard for liberty and justice. In that case you must resist the temptation to use the seemingly available expedients of demagogic mass manipulation, terrorist mass intimidation, and state-worship. Or else you should consistently proceed to a Fascist–National-Socialist form of totalitarian state and a new absolutism.

To me the decisive lesson of German experience seems to be that this is the only possible way of clarifying the essential conditions for the rebirth and defense of the irreplaceable elements in democracy. It may well be that in the process a few of the loudest defenders of democracy and human progress will prove false friends.

BETWEEN CHAOS AND TYRANNY

"Can they remain parliamentary, liberal democracies if they wish to make war efficiently?" doubts Halévy in *L'Ère des Tyrannies*.

But temporary dictatorship is a legitimate expedient of democracy to secure a higher degree of efficiency in emergencies.

Seldom has so much harm been done as by the confusion between the feasible, temporarily necessary concentration of responsibility in a dictatorship within the restrictions of an equitable and democratic state, and the radically different modern tyranny and absolutism. Such confusions are not only understandable, they have also in many cases been deliberately fostered for demagogic purposes as a diversion and a smokescreen. Such blurring not merely of shadings but of fundamental distinctions promotes the political twilight that demagogues of all kinds usually enjoy. To give the collective name of fascism, for instance, to such various attempts as those of Salazar in Portugal, Kemal Ataturk in Turkey, Metaxas in Greece, and Dolfuss in Austria, and put them on a level with National Socialism, requires the rigid outlook of the doctrinarians who purposely shut their eyes to truth because it upsets their positive teachings and beliefs.

Certainly a democracy may preserve under a dictatorship the essential elements of democratic life, and then return without difficulty to the previous forms of democracy after the emergency is over. But despite the apparent preservation of democratic forms there may develop, in the midst of the democratic system, institutions that must infallibly lead to some kind of modern absolutism and tyranny. From them we escape with difficulty, if at all.

I am far from maintaining that this confusion everywhere constitutes deliberate misrepresentation. But the cheap and rigid standards of judgment employed for instance by certain émigrés of various nationalities result in people's disregarding the importance of valuable attempts at a regeneration of democracy, while on the other hand adherents are recruited for measures belonging directly to the arsenal of tyranny.

It is hard to form a sound opinion of the attempts to adapt democracy to the new elements of life, such as were made in Portugal, Austria, Greece, or for that matter in Pilsudski's Poland.

Were they efforts to assimilate the revolution — examples of a great and honorable union between tradition and revolution? Or do they not also present elements of spurious assimilation; are they not postponements of real decision, or artificially induced abortions?

Only a searching examination could yield the answer. But no one has any right to doubt that there has here been a real effort to deal with the decisive problems of the inevitable new future order. To doubt it would be the part of a spiteful demagogue, trying to deny that a regeneration of democracy within certain limits is necessary at all.

In all these groping attempts we must ask not whence the methods come, or what philosophical system they belong to, but only whether they are useful, whether they meet the political difficulties. After all, we should be able to forget the ideological origins and doctrinaire systems to which individual ideas belong, and instead should use without preconceived prejudice anything that will do practical good. If we do so, we may incidentally discover on closer inspection that many expedients can be classed with neoliberalism quite as well as with neocorporativism or neosocialism.

In the grave German crisis even before the National Socialist upheaval it became abundantly clear that the various theories of economic and political doctrine were no longer of any use, and that the problems must be faced much more realistically and with a more open mind than the older generation then in office had done. It seemed time to throw all those principles overboard as excess baggage, and to seek a practical solution for each problem as it came up. It must be admitted that this unorthodox attitude toward all the signs of crisis also had its dangers. Was there any compass left — could we still steer for some port? At all events this absence of doctrine was the soil on which, it must be confessed, the National Socialist slogans of "resolute action" took root in Germany.

Even so there are probably greater advantages in this attitude than in keeping to the old patterns and doctrines, and accepting only what falls within a familiar systematic structure. No real assimilation of the revolutionary forces can ever be achieved in this way. Such assimilation must amount to a refining-down of old systems of ideas, and the creation of new combinations.

What part of the attempts in Portugal, Greece, Poland, Austria and Turkey can we use? We cannot use the attempts, natural enough for weak states staggered by inner turmoil, to regenerate the political structure through affiliation with the army. Such notions prevailed in Poland and even in Germany, until National Socialism ejected the Reichswehr from its position of power. The strict discipline and the fact that the army *was* the state in its final tangible embodiment as power, as a united and unified association of wills, made it tempting to use this regulative force in civilian departments as well. In Germany, furthermore, the army still sustained a certain political continuity, the last remnants of a traditionalism almost entirely extinct.

The mistake in this scheme is not simply the temptation to build the state into a sort of army-camp order, and center its policy on considerations of military expansion, but the fact that all social life then belongs to the state. Everything is centralized and everyone put in uniform by means of a quasi-military discipline that is bound to destroy civil liberties and democratic character.

The contrary attempt, to create a moral authority, making the Christian faith and the church the basis of the social order, unquestionably touches upon the crucial weakness of modern states and societies. But can we restore a lost ethical foundation by decree? Can we compel a Christian life by authoritarian measures? Are we not tempted at last, even if with good intentions, to employ the methods of outward terror for this spiritual end? This signifies completely missing the real purpose of any re-Christianization and any common faith sustained by true conviction. At best we have a new kind of clericalism. A Christian foundation by decree, a forced Christianization, could not produce much better results, in an extreme case, than the enforced world concepts of the existing totalitarian regimes.

Nor is any advance over the existing difficulties to be seen in a state of estates, a state built on corporate bodies. Autonomous bodies may indeed be an addition to the existing democratic organs if they do not become state organs and thus tools for the denomination of economic and social spheres by a centralized state, if they remain the old, true self-governing units. But any corporative orders worked out as yet have been the very opposite — have stood for state subjugation of the last autonomous spheres of social life, and exploitation of these forces for the ends of a new absolutism.

In general we find the mistake of all these attempts in the fact that their tendency is to create a central power rather than a center of superior authority, whose only function would be to adjust

151

differences among interests and autonomous spheres. The countries mentioned, in their attempts at a new order, in general merely transferred authorities to the state, which gradually made the latter the sole and omnipotent power. This is bound to lead to the new absolutism, and eventually to a species of modern tyranny, even though we may admit that some of these states are far from that point, and have managed to maintain an even balance among quite divergent tendencies.

To find a middle road, a road running between chaos and tyranny, was the purpose of these experiments. This was bound to tend toward the creation of a stronger authority, a recourse above parties, whose business it was to preserve the essential substance of democracy, political compromise, the conciliation of interests, and to prevent a majority dictatorship. In tendency, therefore, these experiments do fundamentally belong in the democratic line. In practice they have frequently succumbed to the temptation of totalitarian methods.

MISTAKES IN METHOD

It is fruitless to see only the negative side of the political attempts that finally produced National Socialism in Germany and novel combinations of authority and democracy in the other states mentioned. At present our fate depends not simply on the rightness or wrongness of our aims, but even more on the right or wrong methods we employ. We quarrel over aims, and disagree virtually to the point of civil war about our political visions of the future. But for these various purposes we often use the same means and methods. Then we are surprised that from all our various political starting-points we accomplish scarcely more than one result — the further breakdown of the existing order, with no permanent framework for a new one. We interpret it as a sort of doom of our times that we can only "will" to go in one direction. We none of us gain our ends, but eventually find ourselves in the same morass, no matter what goal we have been aiming at, or where we started from. The answer to this transformation in mid-passage — and National Socialism is not alone in undergoing it — is unsuitable methods of pursuing our aims. The fact that conservative elements in Germany thought they could use National Socialism as a means to arrive at a new traditionalist order, and in every point actually accomplished the opposite of what they had intended, does not prove the inescapability of the fate marked out for us by the mass nature; it is rather the expression of a mistake in means.

Greater liberty cannot be won by total coercion; we cannot shape the masses into a new traditionalist order by organizing a mass revolution; we cannot vanquish Caesarist mass democracy by making it into the actual form of sovereignty. We can never introduce an order built on higher justice by first permitting a great general injustice.

Any cynicism, any unscrupulousness in methods has a disintegrative effect. The means grow too big for their employers, take on an independent life of their own, and rush along the very paths they were designed to avoid. We have here the remarkable automatism of events that is so conspicuous a phenomenon in modern history. It is therefore a disastrous mistake to think oneself dependent on the weapons of one's adversaries, and feel forced to adopt them. Certainly in a contest of infamies the most unscrupulous will set the pace at first. But there is the other, the only effective weapon against infamy of method, namely the method that is different, one that is appropriate to one's purpose. I believe we could have saved ourselves much misfortune by what I might call the accommodation of means to ends.

Forcing a violent solution by material means instead of patiently and painfully undertaking to build up from within — using methods of coercion for an outward order instead of traveling the harder road of slow education — has always been the expedient of people who wanted to see something happen, who were devoured by impatience because things moved too slowly.

Our age is ahead of other ages in the effectiveness of modern coercive methods and the psychological tricks of mass leadership. The effectiveness of organized machinery and mechanism guarantees almost absolute success. Those governing today, once they are in possession of the instruments of power, need no longer regard the masses as an incalculable factor, an unknown quantity. The masses are no longer a danger, but a plastic substance that will assume any desired form under the kneading hands of the expert. This is the seductive temptation. The masses now can scarcely break loose as an untamed force of nature. Their forces can be canalized, and even used advantageously. They can be put to any purpose that a governing class may decide on. Here is an explosive force that will, if used in a suitable machine, drive forward the vehicle of any political ambition with unexampled speed. What a tremendous simplification — how much easier than the difficult manipulation of public opinion in the democracies! How much less complicated than the absolute regimes of the seventeenth and eighteenth centuries! Only one thing is necessary: we must be determined to use the means that will enable us to seduce the masses in this fashion. These means are familiar. There are not only terrorism and violence, there are all the methods of mass provocation, suggestion and intoxication that modern propaganda has taught, and that have stamped the new collective character on the soul of modern society.

Are we not actually bound to use these methods, no matter how degrading it may be? Does not the modern mass condition positively force us to? If we, that is "we" who are convinced that we know what is best for the nation and the future social order — do not do so ourselves, will not others do it instead? Others — the unscrupulous, gangsters, men caring for nothing but their own selfish purposes? Is not the point therefore to act as swiftly as possible in order to anticipate these gangsters? Time flies. We are in fearful danger: for, make no mistake, once the masses are thus subjugated, once a new governing class has firmly established itself and taken possession of the instruments of power, freedom of action is done for; then the path will be irrevocably foreordained. No opposition can struggle against the monstrous modern methods of violence, any more than the masses can. What happens will be irrevocable, impossible of correction.

This is the horrifying part of our situation. The machinery of self-revision that existed in the parliamentary systems through changing government majorities no longer functions. Where it still exists it depends entirely on a tacit agreement of all parties not to use the decisive means of power and mass domination.

How long can the temptation be resisted? Will not moral stamina decrease with each intensification of the crisis, and along with it the suspicion that someone else — the parliamentary opposition or the army, business groups, or no matter who — is taking the final and supreme recourse?

And, people go on to wonder, would not such a seizure of power be in the interests of the masses? People feel that the bad part, after all, is only the abuse of the new methods of dominating and psychologically seducing the masses — abuse for the purpose of subjugating these masses without regard to general aims, simply for the sake of dominion. If, on the contrary, we do it in the interest of the masses themselves, as their trustee, so to speak, for their own advantage, where can be the harm? The maintenance of democracy, in so far as it can be maintained at all, seems to demand this procedure.

In the name of democracy and progress, people conclude, we must have the courage to put democracy partially out of action in order to create a new procedure that will at least make it possible to use the modern instruments of power in the interests of progress, not barbarism. The mass age is irrevocable. Anyone who dreams of returning to older forms of political and social life is a romantic. The new actuality, which has created modern industrial society with its mass leveling, demands the methods and means of domination and propaganda hitherto properly developed, indeed, but wrongfully used, by totalitarian states.

One can argue in this way, and in fact people do. Indeed the most intelligent groups are the very ones that do so — those who have recognized the nature of the new age in one aspect. But they are mistaken nevertheless. This very mistake is the beginning of a disaster that cannot but lead to some self-destructive action, like the "national overturn" in Germany. Any social overturn, if we care to call it so, is bound in the course of further consistent development to succumb to methods that a socialist revolution would not be able to avoid any more than National Socialism has. The destruction is implicit in the very nature of the new methods of domination, and not merely in the political aims. Even though the masses were not, as in Germany, subjugated for warlike expansionist ends, but for a new social order, destruction would be inherent in this subjugation and in the methods of maintaining it.

No doubt people will reply, just as we did to ourselves in Germany when we participated in the National Socialist experiment, that there was nothing else to do. In saying this you take comfort in the reflection that you are merely accepting the masses as they must be accepted. You call things by their right names, and do with a clear conscience what shrewd party demagogues have long done stealthily and with slight gnawings of conscience. Only instead of the party machine we have a new machinery, a greater, more powerful one, from which there is no recourse to any other quarter. The manipulation of public opinion will become somewhat more vigorous; there are limits beyond which criticism simply cannot be tolerated any longer. The extent of enthusiasm, intoxication, soothing, and diversion that the masses need in order to remain in the proper state — people tell themselves — amounts to no more than a sort of hygiene and mass-soul dietetics. The evil and destructive effect, they go on to argue, lies in extremes, in the exaggeration of means that are necessary in themselves.

Only these methods make it possible at last to give back to the masses simple, universal, large, and effective ethical standards of value and action. This, they say, is the only way to lay a solid foundation for a future order capable of supporting a state, a nation, a society. Only thus can wars and stresses be endured — not, as the French example has shown, with the whole tremendously differentiated heritage of our political conventions.

Such considerations bring us to exactly the point where we Germans began our journey to destruction eight, nine, ten years ago. It is not only Rightists, reactionary elements, which succumb to the temptation of these methods, but equally the groups that cannot say enough against the amoralities of a Prussian state and its unscrupulous diplomatic ethics, yet that swear by the same sort of ethics where the realization of their own aims — making mankind happy, a definite order of society — is concerned.

Here we find another effect of the connection between Hegel and Marx. Even in Lenin there are echoes of Hegel's statement that the morally evil is the catalyst, the impulse releasing new creative developments — that it stands for "creative negation." People reassure themselves by the thought that the present age must pass through this creative negation before it can start to build something new.

But "even for a good purpose we must tread the true, not the wrong and dishonest paths," Thomas Aquinas warns us.

THE POLITICAL TEMPTATIONS OF THE PRESENT AGE

It is not in mistaken methods alone, in the exploitation of the masses and the use of their psychological weaknesses, that the political temptation of this age lies — not alone in the "guile" of politics. There is also the temptation to "short-circuit," to furnish an artificial solution.

The typical short-circuit solution consists in rendering revolutionary events unnecessary by forestalling their results. This is not the same as a diversion toward true evolutionary development. On the contrary, such anticipation is possible only by coercive measures. By the resources of outward power we wring out something that could have been lasting only through voluntary change. These forced results lack precisely the virtues of such a true evolutionary answer as real compromise, i.e., a willingness to surrender complete fulfilment of one's own wishes. The good intention of abbreviating the crisis and avoiding costly by-paths is worthless compared to the havoc wrought by the coercive methods.

Matters cannot be left alone after these coercive methods have been used once, as if on the theory that the people need only be helped into the saddle in order to ride by itself. On the contrary, the employment of force to get a result simply means that we cannot stop using force for the consolidation and extension of the results. The statement that this is only a temporary measure, an individual remedy, is one of the disastrous delusions encountered in all these short-circuit solutions.

A further temptation usually appears at this point. The ease with which certain solutions resembling *coups d'etat* at first succeed, misleads people into using the power, once set in motion, for structures and institutions that could never have been achieved through the customary political channels. The temptation of geometrical construction, of rational planning, comes close in the wake of the first use of coercion when we cast off the shackles of convention, supervision and tradition.

It is a despotism of reason that is here established. Robespierre said that liberty was the despotism of reason. But reason is despotism in a far wider sense. It is the despotism of political and economic planning as well as the functioning machinery that permits one to accomplish the altogether impossible — the despotism of machinery, whose functioning leads to self-deception about the possible and the necessary, and thus renders misuse tempting because it still seems to be accomplishing productive work where in reality it is already destroying.

The temptation inherent in the possession of power itself is irresistible. It is a disastrous mistake to think that the debasing of power lies wholly with its possessors, and that in other hands some good might have resulted. Power in the sole possession of one individual or irremovable group corrupts in any case, and leads to the same situations as in the regimes that cynically and openly proclaim power as the sole efficient regulator of human society.

The political temptation of our age, embracing all other temptations, is the temptation of Leviathan.

The old editions of Hobbes' *Leviathan* contain the celebrated illustration depicting the man-god, the mortal god, the multi-man, Leviathan — a man made up of countless men. Is the reference only to the state, the then new absolute state? Why did Hobbes call upon the old magical name Leviathan, the beast from the deep, which will return in the Apocalypse?

Leviathan is the artificial, atheistic order, autocratic, exclusively human, consistently secular, rationalistic. It is the order of Lucifer, claiming to be the goal of the ages, the end of history, the society of the future, the future state — an absolute world order. The temptation of Leviathan is the temptation of a new absolutism. As early as Proudhon it was said that "the simple development of the idea inevitably leads to the conclusion that the ideal of society is absolutism." In vain it would be urged as an excuse that this absolutism was temporary.

Leviathan is the sovereign rule of technology; it is technology grown absolute, not merely "the most decisive anti-Christian force that has yet appeared" (Ernst Juenger). It leads mankind from its previously accustomed organic relations with the surrounding world to an entirely new and artificial creation. Leviathan is efficient planning; it is the god that satisfies the elemental craving for material security. It provides diversion, substitute satisfaction, the intoxication without which the masses' fear for existence threatens to become insupportable. This god is worshiped through the "organizing of enthusiasm" and the training away of the individual self. Collective thinking, the supremacy of state over life, the amusements that enslave are offerings that smell sweet in his nostrils. Just so a new discipline grows up behind the "entertainment" in such methods of "coordination" as radio and film, behind the motions of operating the machine; these means depersonalize man by distracting him from himself. Leviathan is the universal world machine of which mankind are the operatives, and in which the only characterization is "satisfactory or faulty material," where human beings are as interchangeable as the spark plugs in a motor.

5

Leviathan

LEVIATHAN IS THE STATE that concentration of power has made into a *deus mortalis,* a mortal god, which can offer only material security to its citizens. But even Hobbes realized that this state, whatever it bestowed, must win by fear, by terrorism. The Leviathan imparts its measure of earthly security at the price of enslavement, and this not merely of its subjects' bodies and lives, but of minds and souls as well.

Restoration of the union between worldly and ecclesiastical authorities in the broadest sense of the word has been the irresistible course of the historical development in which all the Continental countries have been involved since the Middle Ages. This is the long road away from the medieval plural order. It incorporates the indirect authorities of the autonomous bodies and the domains of self-government and personal rights in one central, uniform administrative machinery. It is "coordination." What National Socialism did under that name was the final, strongest and most consistent expression of an elemental tendency that has been making itself felt since the seventeenth century. The state became once more what it had been in pagan times: the deified embodiment of all human relations.

It is a general tendency for the state to develop toward its most effective and consistent form. The tendency toward consistent reconstruction into a total, absolute machine of domination with an exact technique and exercise of power lay in the very nature of the State as it was developed in the seventeenth century.

Through their conception of the state, Bolshevism and Fascism are merely developing the totality of power in a new way through the medium of the new reality created by technology and the rise of the masses. But this development occurs perforce wherever a modern power machine arises to exercise leadership over the entire life of a social group according to an inclusive plan. Therefore every form of total mobilization, all war economy and all political and economic planning on a grand scale are in danger of becoming a form of the new absolute state or an absolute society or a partial absolutism. Identity of the absolute state and total society is the characteristic final result of this development.

All the great centralized state and social machineries serving for total war mobilization, or any other mobilization, no matter how good and proper the motives and aims of their management may be, are bound to end in the absolutism of the modern Leviathan. The temptation is grave because any great machinery for leadership is far superior to the traditionalist, historical, cumulative orders. This is true, no matter what may be said against such machinery, because of the clear, efficient articulation and coordination of work, which saves time, pains and energy. That which may be achieved in this fashion is so tremendously superior that limitations of the individual's personal sphere must take second place by comparison. This, however, brings the sphere of individual rights into dangerous conflict with the sphere of alleged general welfare.

As regards the much criticized development of a special "state ethics" in Germany, according to which the concepts of private morality do not hold for the state, of course there is a perfectly obvious argument to show why the amorality proper to the state is not permissible for other institutions of society. Then, naturally, every sort of public right and good faith becomes illusory. Thus we have here too a logical development inherent in the thing itself. For that matter, even Hobbes recognized the distinction between *public reason* and *private reason*. The really dangerous development, however, is that wherein no such distinction can be made because no private reason is allowed; the private sphere can no longer be tolerated. This means, then, that only state reasons of expediency are valid even in personal relationships, and personal morality must not be allowed to interfere with them. This is precisely our present situation.

Modern state and social absolutism is bound to inhibit any private inner sphere for the single individual. Very likely freedom of thought may not be prohibited by decree; instead, absolutism will practically exterminate it through the new technique of propaganda and mass suggestion. It will not deny the individual's right to a private sphere of life, it will entangle him in such a network of public duties and rights, activities and amusements, that he ceases to exist as an individual.

Fundamentally the old absolute state was a policeman. It desired nothing beyond public peace, safety and order. The new absolute state requires infinitely more. In order to shape and maintain its new rational order it must educate a new type of humanity. It must "plan" a new corps of civil servants. It can leave no unsupervised gaps in legal and state life. Public justice is at the same time custom. Therefore the absolutism plans custom, and with custom, the man. It creates no personalities; it tolerates none. For personalities are always flaws and hindrances in an exact process. Therefore it creates types. It robs man of his "immortal soul." It cannot but be anti-Christian — it is Antichrist.

But is the security afforded by the mortal god, Leviathan, worth such sacrifices? Does it offset terror and unfreedom? Today, as three hundred years ago, the craving for a collective security, a social and political security, is what brings in absolutism.

THE ENTICEMENT OF LEVIATHAN

Men do not obey terror alone; they also require some hope. Leviathan governs by political enticement. It entices by guaranteeing a security that will eliminate fear; it entices with the promise of an earthly paradise. Its bait for the masses is a secular millennium, the picture of an ideal society or of perpetual peace and an equitable order. The fear factor plays a great part in the development of the new absolutism today. We have a permanent crisis, with increasing material worries, and fear for existence on the part of masses that no longer know the spiritual surcease of the transcendental. Even Condorcet, as early as 1793, portrayed in his *Esquisse d'un Tableau Historique* the "goal of humanity,"

166

which becomes the test of all public political and social questions, and plays its part as a war aim today, in the socialist upheaval before the *coup d'état* in Germany, and indeed everywhere, avowedly or secretly, in "Strength through Joy" with its "rejoice in life." The goal of humanity thus described is security, prolongation of life, comfort, hygiene, draining of the swamps of the subconscious and the remnants of a mythical age of primitive fear; psychoanalysis instead of religion; canalization of the natural instincts; the destruction of spiritual by sexual love; the covering over of death as something indecent; absolute materialism. This combination of temptations keeps bringing the socialist-rationalist wing of our civilization into Leviathan's field of force. Only the absolute state, where society and state are one, and there is no liberty even to think and feel in secret, can bestow complete security and an earthly paradise based on reason.

No matter whether we demand it as Condorcet did or, like Robert Ley, as "Strength through Joy" or — not in the same breath, of course — even as "the social functions," it is at bottom the same: a hope, a distraction, a myth. Enticement is held out not only to the imagination of the masses, but equally to the reason of the intellectuals. Leviathan lures by the very logic of its order, by the reasonableness and efficiency of its principles.

Even the state as it arose in the seventeenth century is not the expression of a previously existing natural order more or less reflected in all the state forms; instead it is an artificial, a rational human creation. Rational efficiency and the decisive factor of power are what determine the state. Instead of being based on a "contract," it now expresses an actual power situation, which it regulates by a rational technique. The rationality, the efficiency of its existence, is what gives it its indisputable superiority over the traditional forms of a historical state.

The modern "heroic" man is attracted by this Leviathan in quite a different way. To him it is the infallible machine of sub-jugation. With it he can keep the masses in a state of depend-ence. Even Leviathan needs a ruling elite which, for its own part, is above fear as a means for its own subjugation, and equally above earthly bliss as an element in a way of life. This, incidentally, is most impressively stated in Dostoievsky's *The Grand Inquisitor*. For if everyone in the perfect paradise yearned for the same hap-piness, and wanted to go shopping every day in the "petty-happi-ness department store," there would be no one left to do the hard work of leadership, without which even the Leviathan state cannot exist. This new master class rules by giving the masses what they crave, namely, security and an earthly paradise. Left and Right wings, Utopians and adherents of modern tyranny, join in this gift to the masses. What distinguishes them is that one side uses as a means what the other proclaims as an end.

If one can give room to all these ideas of a possible, permanently practicable, world order, then perhaps the road that Hitler has chosen is after all the rational one, instead of the road Marx fore-saw. I believe criticism must go much further than it has yet been pushed against National Socialism. Such criticism must, indeed, also include the whole hundred years' history of Marxism as well as the new state absolutism. Hitler is right when he goes beyond Marxist ideas in establishing his giant absolute state. If we expropriate the whole world of national states, incorporate them in a monstrous state collective through a series of revolutionary wars, and then, possessing the impregnable sovereign power, build up the inner social and economic structure on to a uniform rational plan, it is certainly more efficient and more promising than the opposite method, of beginning with a social revolution.

Nothing is more prejudicial to a clear judgment of the great historical crisis than the unconscious or even deliberate dishonesty with which the political leaders of all parties conceal most of their aims. Revolution starts with undefined fronts and self-delusion about what one really wants. I am convinced that the overwhelming majority of those fighting against the forces of nihilist destruction today have the proper feeling, and are offering their lives in an elemental recognition of the mortal danger to the future of humanity. But is that enough?

Not even the unimpaired ruggedness of a people such as the British, its common sense, its feeling for proportion and limitations, may be enough to confront these temptations, confusions and enticements successfully without other aid.

ATHALIE

Chance has thrown Racine's *Athalie* in my way. I read it in our shelter among the sleeping French captains, and am following the tragedy with growing excitement. It is like a key to these questions that incessantly occupy our minds. Across the centuries one sees how closely things hang together in our marvelous Europe. The play is a plain disavowal of the monistic absolutism of the seventeenth-century state; it is a judgment upon a world order that sees its center in itself alone. All human order is plural — this is the hidden lesson. Monism is apostasy from the god in man; it is bound to end in tyranny.

Who will vanquish the beast from the deep, "Who is able to make war with him?" says the Apocalypse. If one were to answer *a mixed government,* it would sound like a witticism. Yet perhaps this is the briefest, the most realistic answer.

The objections made to the irresponsible government of "indirect forces" are sound; the objections that can be urged against plural state structures are sound. Wherever people believe they need a strong state in order to escape from the battle of interests, from crises and latent revolution, it is precisely the elimination of indirect forces that they have seen as the means to regenerate public life. We ourselves once espoused this error; we believed we might safely venture the inconsistency of looking with one eye toward a strong monistic state, and with the other toward a great free commonwealth of autonomous members, a new "Holy Empire."

"La République une et indivisible" of the French Revolution was the logical continuation of Richelieu's absolute monistic state. For that matter the Prussian state, today rather stupidly made the scapegoat for all the infamies of National Socialist policy, likewise has the roots of its absolutism in the seventeenth century, in Hobbes' *Leviathan.* In regard to the German Republic, which was created as the opposite solution to the Prussian state, we must distinguish between the written constitution of a model liberal, equitable state, and the definitely contrasting actual development, even here, toward a centralized, absolutist Leviathan state.

170

This too is proof of an automatism of development leading concentrically from all starting points toward absolutism, even against the will of the guiding and planning personalities. The temptation toward such a development arises both in respect to aims like the social state and in the effort to remove politics and statesmanship from the field of warring subjective interests and "make them objective."

Here too we can cast back to the seventeenth century. As that century sought beyond theological disputation for a neutral area where there would be objectivity and order in tangible factors, so we today are trying to escape from the jungle of political fictions to a political economy of objective missions removed from doctrine. Such concrete problems always have a severely limited number of practicable solutions.

It was not only that the parties as direct forces simply complicated the course of administration and formed a disturbing element in the perfected administrative machinery. With this combination of social pluralism, party pluralism, a backward territorial pluralism, and the pluralism of the economic bodies, how could a state survive and guarantee an objective solution of the public difficulties? The parties and other indirect forces were obstacles in the path to complete administrative mechanization. They endangered prompt performance of imperative work, and hence helped make the crises more acute.

In *L'Ere des Tyrannies,* Halévy tells how Sidney Webb explained to him that the future would belong to a great administrative nation, which would govern through bureaus, and how order would be maintained by gendarmes. As against technification of politics and administration, where "the machine" rules, the work of parties is mere waste of time and energy. Here too, then, we arrive at the "mortal god," Leviathan. Leviathan knows no indirect forces — nothing but the one indivisible power and responsibility, administered by a great, self-contained hierarchy. These efforts toward "objectivity" bring representatives of the most diversified political tendencies together with a bureaucracy that plans a new absolutism, an "impartial state."

The demand for objectivity, for objective justice, is sensible and right. Every problem has an optimum solution to be found only through expert knowledge of the subject, not through the game of politics or compromises of interests. This logically brings one to the office state, to bureaus, to state technocracy. But if we do not want altogether to eliminate the indirect forces in a rising absolute state, we use the expedient of replacing parties by a single party. If we keep the parties from their political dabbling and intrigue, dictated by private interests, we have apparently taken a great forward step in rendering politics objective.

The lone party comes into being as a sort of crammer for total absolutism, with the ostensible purpose of acting as a second, supervising authority parallel to the actually decisive, omnipotent state. Is the lone party really a trustee of the people? The function assigned to it by Hitler has been not simply that of a directive machine but also that of a safety-valve, a corrective to authoritarian volition, the engine of a continuous plebiscite. Caesarism under plebiscite, accordingly, is still a sort of democratic variety of Leviathan state, not yet its ultimate extreme.

Athalie is no infamous tyrant; she is an absolute ruler intelligently and responsibly trying to do the best thing for her people in her own way. In a human and secular sense she is a noble figure, the very archetype of the strong, self-reliant human being who needs no gods. She is not a tyrant in the regular sense — not an egotistically masterful tyrant. In a human and rational sense she is right to rule as she does rule.

Leviathan is alluring because its principles are rationally correct and solid, since they serve "the greatest good of the greatest number."

But is not the state the very thing that must be got out of the way? Must we not break loose from the state in order to reach new forms of association? Is not this the chief task of the future? In the Middle Ages we have an institutional framework for the forces of public order, but no central and firmly organized state. Is not the dissolution of the state during the baroque period and under nationalist Jacobinism the preliminary to a new order, a European commonwealth? At any rate the concept of a nation must be separated from that of a state, as well as from the duties of the social functions. Great Britain for her part has long since gone beyond the rank of a national state, if she ever was a state in the Continental sense. It would be catastrophic if in the war England were to catch up belatedly with this Continental stage of development, and as a result the Empire's national-state character were to be intensified.

A European or universal commonwealth cannot be a super-state, a giant Leviathan; it must develop a different form of union among national, social and economic societies, preserving the cultural and social heritages and administrative usages of the various nations. It would be fruitless to insist on the basis of a league of sovereign states, which would be distinguished from the earlier League of Nations only by the fact that a few rights of member states would be abdicated to a central authority. And a central state of European dimensions would be a misfortune because it must necessarily absorb all the destructive tendencies of absolutism, even if it were a super-state for the social functions.

The state for the social functions: a marvelous slogan that might effectively replace the concepts of the liberal state, the equitable state, the impartial state, the hero state. But are the social functions the business of a centralized state? The moment they are centrally organized and form a centrally managed state, this order, planned in the social spirit, succumbs to the enticements of Leviathan quite as readily as the other centralized orders. Such functions would become further means for concentrating the public power. They would be used as methods of domination. They would degenerate into arrangements by the central power to maintain or extend its influence.

In *Athalie* the dualism that determines medieval public life is held up as the proper order in contrast to the monism of a pagan state absolutism. This dualism cannot be revived. But in its place we shall have to have a balance of several forces, which will be the more necessary the further we extend the limits of a universal order.

Leviathan, the beast from the deep, is not simply Hitler. It is not merely National Socialism, the totalitarian regimes, modern tyranny. It is rather the ultimate consequence of man's fight for

174

liberty; he sets up his own order, an opposing order to the divine one revealed to mankind. It is progress leagued with barbarism. It is emancipation turning to total slavery. It is the earthly immortality of man through a collective human being, a mass man, a termite humanity.

6

The Redemption of Democracy

I AM TAKING a walk through the City. Elm Court in the Temple has been struck at just the spot where we spent so many absorbing hours; the precious library is destroyed. Only recently we were inspecting the splendid order and arrangement of this unique legal collection. The marvelous hall of the Middle Temple is demolished — a room where the atmosphere of Shakespeare still lived. Pieces of an old, unbroken tradition are destroyed one after another; Holborn, close to us, presents staggering scenes of destruction. Memories of the last war come to life again.

Quand même! Things go forward; there is no flagging of spirit to be seen.

G. has had a bomb drop on his newest quarters. There is no safety anywhere; disaster lies in wait at every corner. Even this Little France, the secret spot in Kensington, a remembrance of the French émigrés in the days after the Great Revolution, has been hit. Ch. has been saved by a miracle; the façade of his house is simply blown away.

Things are disturbed again. The day is dull and lowering.

177

The anti-aircraft fire starts early, and is heavier than it has been the last few nights.

While I am taking my walk today two bombs fall without warning, disagreeably close by, and everyone takes to cover. For a short time we stand in a shelter along with taxi drivers and women shoppers. There is not an ill-humored word — nothing but jokes and laughter.

The question on whether Hitler can still invade England absorbs everyone I talk to. In June I was firmly convinced that Hitler would not land. The unfailing bombardments seemed to be only diversion maneuvers, steps in connection with the blockade. Apparently the main line of action was in the Mediterranean, in the Near East. Oil seemed to be the point — oil, the cleavage of the Empire, occupation of key points, and last but not least Russia, the unvarying goal — to dissolve which and absorb it in their own empire remains an aim that the National Socialists have never surrendered.

Today I am not so sure. Perhaps these attacks are really mere diversion maneuvers on a grand scale, but perhaps the whole idea is simply to tie down one part of the fleet in the Mediterranean, and the other part in the home ports, in order to strike with all available U-boats at Great Britain's exposed flank, her merchant marine. At any rate the spectacle we see today is no longer a single engagement, no longer simply lightning war upon an isolated adversary; it is a huge and varied enterprise, whose real aim is the political collapse of Great Britain. The collapse is to be so engineered that groups other than those now in political control can still make a so-called compromise peace.

178

A compromise peace would be a victory for Hitler — a victory of revolution.

In attempting here to sketch a few outlines of our great crisis, I might say I was trying to characterize the temptations of our age as I have felt and striven to overcome them. In a situation like ours anything one may say is a personal confession, and this is all that matters. This age lacks the balance for objective portrayal, which in any case would far exceed my powers. The personal character of this meditation is not altogether a mere makeshift for lack of maturity. In an age where the continuity of historical developments seems to be broken off, any attempts to tie the snapped threads must be made by individuals. Confidence in the return of an almost extinct faith in the higher destiny of man is not kindled by words, in the lecture halls and forums of public opinion, but by the lonely struggles of each one of us who is earnestly striving to overcome in his own soul the temptations of his own time.

Perhaps this war will become meaningless as a war, as a destructive passage at arms. It will keep its meaning, indeed will begin to reveal it at all, only as a struggle of ideas and values — as a struggle of two orders: the great world civil war, which will end some day with a great peace.

The two tasks that should occupy us are those of clarifying the inner world of values and clarifying the outer elements of fate and social order. Either is possible only in connection with a rebirth of democracy. Let us admit to ourselves the downfall of the old democracy. We must recognize the causes of this downfall, and hence of the rise of the totalitarian powers, before there can be any regeneration. Those who wanted to throw the whole democratic order overboard as mere ballast were wrong; but those who confused this order with its ineffectual institutions were equally wrong.

A friend asks me for a continuation of the *Revolution of Nihilism,* or, as the English title reads, *The Revolution of Destruction.* It would seem natural to counter this Revolution of Destruction with a Revolution of Reconstruction; certainly this is the problem. But is a revolution what is needed? Would not that be to repeat the mistake that we young conservatives in Germany made when we coupled regeneration with revolutionary methods? This was a mistake made even by such a man as Hugo von Hofmannsthal, the great Austrian poet who created the name and idea of a *conservative revolution.* There is no such thing as a revolution of reconstruction. There is only painful, persevering work with individual tasks as a starting point.

In the end we cannot really wish the mere victory of one doctrine or another, one theoretical system or another. Instead we must hope that every useful part of the socialist, corporative or liberal adjuncts will be included in a basically individualistic and liberal structure. How much should be included, how strictly this essentially liberal economy and society will have to be restricted by a legal framework, is something to be decided not by theoretical notions, but by two considerations alone: first, economic and social health and successful functioning; second, improvement of general living conditions. In short, at bottom, practice will decide how much of the desirable is at the same time possible.

And so the formula that may produce renewed health at the end of the present turmoil will be a fairly complicated one. The day of patent solutions and simplifications is gone. We shall have to learn and accept a little of everything. The simple slander applied in the past to everything that was "alien to the system" is a luxury, although we shall have to keep asking ourselves whether a given measure does not possess the quality, already ascribed to several, of inducing a harmful automatism. The moment we allow central interference outside a legal, universal work of reform, we are choosing a path that must be sharply watched if it is not to lead to tyranny.

Among the imperishable treasures forming the essence of democracy is the separation and definition of a personal, private sphere of life beyond reach of public power, an inner world as against an outer world. Possibly we may have to draw sharper distinctions than heretofore. The distinction itself cannot be set aside. It is indispensable if man is not to lose his character as a moral being. It is also essential to recognize that there is and must continue to be a superiority of the spirit over the outward being.

The old democracies function at all now only because they are living on a final sublimation of inner values — on this very superiority of the inner over the outer sphere. Perhaps we may say more concretely that they are living on nothing but routine. In the long run, at any rate, one cannot go on living on mere outward conventions unless they are backed up by a conviction that they are right and necessary, and unless there is an ethical basis to support their observance with the arguments of moral conviction. An order of human society can be maintained without coercion only so long as there lives in it a generally valid image of man. Is such an image of man possible without a divine purpose?

Anyone who has been active in practical politics and the profession of state administration knows that no one ever has time to apply a strict standard of judgment to practical questions so long as he is actually busy with them. It is the tragi-comedy of our political life that the chasm between the abstract and the political never closes. On one hand political science loses itself in abstraction; on the other practice remains crude and blind, and is illumined but rarely by scholarly judgments or calm reflection. This is of advantage to politics, the old politicians declare, and detrimental to the common good, as science says, because one never gets beyond a certain level of rough approximation.

The most tragic feature is that those in positions of political leadership find no time, so long as they are occupied with the job, to profit by the studies of the political and intellectual situation that are constantly being made. Thus the leaders are always using the intellectual armaments of a world already overtaken and outworn. There is a constant discrepancy between the actual problems and the conceptions of them that the leaders continue to hold. The longer leading statesmen are in power, and the greater the speed with which a crisis develops, the further they lag behind their times. In the end they come to see only the rear view, never the true countenance, of all the problems that race ahead of them. They think in old categories and conceptions; whereas what the present age needs is a rethinking of our political categories. Without it we are in danger of ending in meaninglessness.

NEW CATEGORIES

We are all émigrés. Émigrés from our beliefs and concepts, which seem inalterable to us only because we are used to them. We are emigrating from the rigid systems of thought which seemed dependable to us because they were adequate to our former life. They are adequate no longer.

We need a new articulation of the political language, of political nuances. We must get away from the old connections and divisions — away from the distinction between liberal and conservative, bourgeois and labor, tradition and revolution. What overthrew the political forces of the Right, if not the fact that they failed to see the necessity for a regeneration, and wanted only to survive and to outlive themselves? This is something that might be called conservative Jacobinism, which, in the words of Bernanos, sees monarchy and the church as nothing but a double extension of the gendarmerie. Such a combination of opposites as this reactionary Jacobinism, the alliance of social reaction with the methods of revolutionary terrorism, is not what we mean. But neither do we mean revolutionary democracy. As if there could be any such thing — as if after this last, ultimate revolution any revolution could mean anything!

If we turn against centralization in the state, against the absolutism of the whole, we do not want to get in exchange partial absolutisms, false pluralities that merely demand rights in the state and in society without carrying any of the responsibility for the whole. We are not thinking of such doctrines, either, nor of any eclecticism of theories.

The nuances, not the broad doctrines, will be important in the regeneration. It is necessary to advance beyond the catchwords of the nineteenth century, whether they be the struggle between capital and labor or between liberty and equality. There is no definite answer to our difficulties; there is something much more modest, but far more solid in the long run. If coming events force us to dissolve the connection between the democratic order and nationalism, and to surrender the idea of national democracy, what we must put in their place will not be a union of socialism and democracy, that is the idea of social democracy. For in that case we would still be enmeshed in the rival ideas of the nineteenth century. Instead we might develop the idea of a corporative democracy, except that here associations of thought immediately arise to make a new synthesis impossible, instead of facilitating it. But what I mean to express by such a formulation is not actual opposition to the "national" or "social" concept, but a refusal to connect them with a state order. Both national democracy and social democracy have sought embodiment in strong, centralized, homogeneous state forms. Both are based on the principles of the republic one and indivisible; whereas there should be an attempt at a new shape that would range national and social forces as independent spheres, and then would unite them as corporate bodies in a common plural order.

But the language used in the struggle behind us is misleading. The direct expression cannot be used. We must begin by trying to clarify our ideas in order to find a terminology that will be generally understood. The progress of future developments beyond any tendencies toward state *socialism* or state *nationalism* must not be allowed to fail through obscure terminology. It is also a matter of course that it must not stray, for instance, into state *corporatism*. The difficulty of understanding is that the monistic state, which we are accustomed to take for granted as an essential of public order, should not be taken for granted at all; it is the product of a historical development that has to all appearances reached its end.

If this is the case, however, we must not look for the key points in the regeneration of democracy where democracy itself tried to take shelter — in a centralized, uniform, monistic state. That effort produced a sort of state democracy. The very concept of democracy flatly contradicts the idea of the state. Democracy can never regard its relations to a state form, or its embodiment in one, as anything but a compromise. The roots of Western European democracy are in the guilds of the Middle Ages, in the organs of self-government, in the corporate bodies with their own codes. Modern democracy since the eighteenth century has been a compromise of these democratic forces with the powers of absolutism, a century older, which formed an indivisible, omnipotent, homogeneous state with uniform law and centralized administration.

Any attempt to return to old situations and forms would be silly. We need, not this, but clarification: we need to know what parts of established democracy suit democracy's true nature, and what parts have been grafted on in a historical process by connection with other factors such as a chaotic, disintegrating society and the absolutist state.

Democracy, which was alive as the articulated form of society long before the emancipation of the bourgeoisie, was at first exclusively associated with the bourgeoisie. Later identified with a society in constant movement, it assumed a one-sided shape that does not directly accord with its nature. Democracy grew in an articulated society; it is essentially alien to the absolute, centralized state as well as to the shapeless, spineless society of the mass age. It is therefore difficult — indeed, strictly speaking, impossible — to integrate the masses directly in a democratic form. Masses and democracy are mutually exclusive opposites. The concomitants of the masses are tyranny and the absolute state. If democracy is to be preserved, it is necessary to articulate the masses anew.

It is easy for us to succumb to the optical illusion of interpreting as the true nature of democracy the mere historical circumstances of an age during which this democracy became the determining principle of public life. In these circumstances there is just as much of the alien, of the obstacles that democracy had to overcome, as there is of true, essential democracy.

Democracy, we therefore conclude, cannot be identified with the forms and principles of a state whose trend is toward absolutism, whether through the personification of a nation or of a social class. Democracy is not to be regenerated as a centralized state, but through the creation of new domains of autonomy, which may perhaps constitute the organs of a new sort of commonwealth of the future.

186

This sort of thing cannot be decreed. Such a development can come to life only as it is applied to practical problems, and can thus be fostered as it grows by clarification of ideas. But have we not got the elements of this new order, these domains of autonomy, already? Is it not our task rather to help them develop a proper consciousness of themselves as entities, and to prevent the renewal of democracy from being sought where it can never flourish, namely in a centralized, bureaucratic state?

We should look for supplementary, new forms of democratic life among the great corporate bodies, the "indirect forces" of the present age — the unions, the business corporations, the social services, the great, intellectual institutions, and of course as always in parliament, the institution of political parties.

In the present crisis we must take inventory of all the forces making for a conservative way of life, and there must be a new articulation of conservatism. Liberalism as well as socialism is conservative today, not merely in the formal sense that both have something to preserve and defend against the assault of universal nihilism, but in the positive sense that all these political principles, as Western regulative ideas, are indissolubly connected with the preservation of Western Europe. This is the focus for a new synthesis of our political forces. Such a synthesis is possible so long as none of its constituent elements develops into a "partial absolutism," and as long as it lays no claim to exclusiveness — that is, so long as each of these forces behaves as an *adjunct* to order, but not as the principle of domination for a doctrinaire structure.

New political and intellectual coin is minted not by the idea of a revolution, or of a geometrically constructed revolution, or one of social justice, or of a world order, but by the idea of Western European tradition. This tradition embraces the entirety of life, and not merely *homo oeconomicus,* not merely the social sphere. Such an entirety is impossible without an evaluation of life that leads to the transcendental level. It is the sum of the upbuilding forces of Western Europe. It includes the irrational forces, the forces of historical continuity, of tradition in the narrowest sense, the tendencies toward stabilization, permanence, endurance. It includes the forces of private life, even private property.

We are in process of moving out of the familiar household furnishings of our political judgments and distinctions. Few people indeed are capable of realizing how much we shall have to leave behind. Most of what is argued today still falls short of the line that we must cross over. It is conceived in antiquated categories. I am not deluded into thinking that even what is said in these pages is the thing we need, nor what we expect on the far shore.

GRANDEUR AND MISERY OF EMIGRATION

To live as an émigré is hard, but not without its greatness. Still less does it lack its degradations and its own special pettiness. One gains perspective, perceives new relations. Being released from habit, one corrects the one-sided judgments resulting from habitual trains of thought. Perhaps one is enabled to judge more fairly; perhaps one's judgment hardens, and the wish to be fair disappears. As an émigré one may grow smaller, because he is deprived of the supports and scenery of his familiar theater of life, and must play his solo part in a strange land. Why waste words upon the misery of emigration, which is always the same? Where the mangers are empty the horses bite one another, as country people say. Misery and an unsatisfied craving for respect explain many disagreeable aspects of all émigré groups; but *one* greatness none can take from them. Theirs is the call and the voice to be among the leaders in the reshaping of an intellectual world.

Is this vocation truly theirs? It is theirs if they will relinquish the comforting mirage of an early victorious return to the old country; if they give up their claims of being destined personally to direct the future order, and through the experiences of exile to regenerate the country they have left behind. This is not the vocation of the émigrés; theirs is far humbler, more useful — to help with a future understanding, a clarification of antiquated ideas; to form ties, to clear away mistaken judgments. People who have had to leave their native land in times like these stand outside of nations and states; they stand, too, outside of set views and doctrines, or at least they should. They are the perfect intermediaries, if they understand their mission rightly. They will be capable of inestimable service if they can restrict their personal aspirations.

In the last war the men who formed the new national states went abroad. Something of the old romance of the nineteenth-century nationalist conspiracies still lingered about them. The masses were trained from birth to the old ideas of the battle for liberty and independence, as when the Poles, for instance, fought behind all the barricades of liberty against absolutist oppression. This romantic atmosphere justified the political struggle of émigrés in the eyes of the masses who bore the burdens of occupation or the tide of battle sweeping over them during the last war.

Today things have changed. Today these masses will not look to the émigrés; instead they will ask who has borne the real brunt of these years of oppression — who has been in real mortal danger, who has made the greater personal sacrifices for deliverance.

That is how people will talk, and not in Germany alone. I am by no means sure that at least this much is not true, that we who have not been in our own countries during this period will never be able to represent them again. But even if it is not our mission to return to our country in a sealed railroad car, there to prepare a revolution and "to come into power with it," we have a higher duty: to balance possibilities against necessities, to work toward the new order as trustees of our nation, and to clear the obstacles from the path of the new life. We must work toward the new life, toward a readiness to redraw the frontiers of our existence and to find for our strength the order that will not paralyze but inspire it.

Here I must make good a sin of omission. In emphasizing what proves to need change, I have not spoken of the priceless survival as I must in order to prevent misunderstanding. It would ill become one in this liberal country to overlook the enduring forces of liberalism and their importance for future developments. Enlightenment, clarification, criticism, constructive doubt, and emancipation will always be needed, precisely because there is no definite general, unchangeable static order of humanity, but only a perpetual approximation to an ideal condition.

Instead of a harmful element, liberalism is a beneficial corrective, except when as a matter of principle it dissolves all bonds and eats away all tradition — that is, except when it too lays claim to exclusiveness, and is not satisfied with the role of one traditional element among many. Only liberalism as a substitute for religion is intellectually destructive; only a liberalism unwilling to concede the limits of its activity (formerly set by the restricted capacity of a rudimentary technology and by individual responsibility for the community) is economically destructive.

My other sin of omission concerns parliamentarism. Is it outdated as the political instrument of democracy?

The very opposite is the case. The more evident the extent of the universal crisis becomes, the more urgent is the necessity for strengthening the irreplaceable function of parliamentarism. Through every conceivable change in the outer and inner forms of the community, the parliamentary constitution will remain the one expression of democracy that can lay claim to universal validity. It is the form of lasting compromise, which will become more necessary than ever if the centralized states arrive at a looser, plural form.

If here I put the concept of tradition and historical continuity in the foreground of regeneration, I do so because I believe that the most radical revolution in history cannot be overcome by a still more radical revolution, but only by returning to the productive and lasting forces of our civilization — that is, unless we actually wish to flee from the confines of the present civilization into a new cultural era. He who desires this, indeed, is hearkening to another call. He is a Utopian, for a new civilization cannot be "desired," it grows up. It cannot be anticipated, it cannot be planned.

Socialism as well as liberalism belongs to this complex of Western European tradition. This cannot be often enough repeated, because socialism has been the show-piece of every revolution in the past 150 years. It has grown rather old in the process. As a European and Western tradition it goes far back among the deepest roots of our civilization. "Save when there shall be no poor among you," even Moses says (Deuteronomy 15: 4). It has never ceased to be one of the strongest elements in Western society. Need we have a revolution, a renewed upheaval, in order to enunciate this Western tradition more strongly and vitally? Do we not, on the contrary, need tranquil, collective, patient development?

One mission the émigrés certainly have not — to become the shock troops of a revolution. Such ideas seem to me to belong to the war of 1914–1918, not the war of 1939, just as do the notions of trench warfare, of rigid, independent sectors on the front. It is the task of the émigrés to fulfil the intellectual conditions for the patient and purposeful work on which a fruitful future depends. This is an unspectacular occupation, but it accords far better with our situation than any claim to represent some future government.

Here nothing is more inopportune than outworn antipathies and antiquated prejudices. It must be our purpose to consolidate our ideas as components of one single, new, common, greater tradition, instead of reckoning up the mistakes of the past as if we were not all equally responsible and equally guilty of mistakes.

Tradition is not merely a feudal stage property that we have brought down with us to this latter day, but an active element that, like the labor movement with its great institutions, embodies living forces. New elements in historical life keep arising and becoming part of tradition, even though but a moment ago they still seemed revolutionary. This is the only way I can see the new conservatism. Today is no longer the time for the workers to talk revolutionary jargon; they should speak the language of a responsible partner in the community. Democracy is a balance of varying forces; democracy is decentralization, and not simply formal separation of powers. Above all, democracy is the continual development of tradition. The time is past when democracy was considered equivalent to radicalism.

7

The Mystery of Iniquity

"THE MYSTERY of iniquity doth already work," writes the Apostle (II Thessalonians 2: 7). Indeed there is a mystery about this iniquity and its workings "with all power and signs and lying wonders," and its "deceivableness of unrighteousness." People whom you would call neither good nor bad, ordinary people, change suddenly. You thought you knew them; you believed you were familiar with their weaknesses, but with their good sides as well; they were human, with their contradictions, good companions perhaps, good-natured, helpful. All at once they begin to change. They acquire a new face; their features become mask-like. Something alien governs them, speaks with their accents. Their voices grow shrill, their eyes staring. New beings approach you; you recognize them only by their old suits, perhaps by the gestures with which they throw away their cigarettes.

Nothing shocked me more profoundly than the visible change in acquaintances and friends whom I thought I knew, when they came under the spell of the National Socialist system. Good people, as far as human beings are ever good, seemed subject to new appetites. My fellow-farmers, honest and upright, pious, God-fearing, if one may call it that, who could never have brought themselves to do a dishonest act — all at once you find them unscrupulous, dishonorable, taking advantage of the weak. They acquire new habits, take mistresses, grow domineering. They gamble, live beyond their means, sink from level to level, and finally become vile scoundrels who think nothing of tormenting, robbing and murdering those weaker than themselves.

This was my experience with a number of my acquaintances, people whom you could have called anything but weak characters, people who came to National Socialism out of decent motives, or who joined hesitantly, critically, with reservations, because they were horrified by the strange element in the movement. I have seen it happen to former socialists and nationalists, liberals and conservatives, this transformation, this deceivableness of up-righteousness. They gave the impression of men possessed. They were no longer themselves. Their alteration of character verged on split personality, on schizophrenia. I do not know whether it is possible from the medical standpoint to assume something like an epidemic and collective form of schizophrenia. I would be more inclined to see the mystery of iniquity, the work of an "Evil," metaphysical in origin, behind the transformation that seems to have come over the whole German nation.

Something not so obviously present in the other totalitarian regimes plays a part in National Socialism. Only National Socialism hints at the true character of the beast from the deep — the character that Hobbes distinctly felt and tried to indicate when he gave the name *Leviathan* to his absolute state. The modern attempts at a new, consistent absolutism are partly expedients to delay the breakdown of society. But for National Socialism the Leviathan order is not a means to an end, but the end itself. The National Socialists subjugate men not in order to give them a new order, but in order to rule over them. They have no aims but one: power and dominion. They have no gods but this earthly god, Leviathan. They have no doctrines to put into effect, no Utopian order to be established with its help. To them the true nature of Leviathan is revealed as the mystery of iniquity.

Only through National Socialism do we see the anti-human and anti-Christian aspect of this whole attempt to establish a purely secular order. The secular order seems to be founded on coercion and rational planning, and thus perhaps pretends to bestow a secure, reasonable and expedient order upon mankind, but in reality it snatches humanity into a realm of life where it is bound to succumb to this deceivableness of unrighteousness.

Rosenberg calls the National Socialist movement a "revolution of instinct." There could be no more apt description. Instinct grows revolutionary, the bonds of civilization are burst. The primitive instinct of man as an animal being rises through the intervening civilized layer into consciousness. The refinement of spirit achieved by thousands of years' training of the human race is undone. This is the revolution back to the "emotions that make one strong," — cruelty, hardness, pitilessness, masterfulness, greed for power, pleasure. It is no longer merely literary, as it was thirty years ago; it is reality. What Hitler hinted in conversations years ago is followed out. A generation is growing up that can be called only diabolically mistrained — a generation to whom everything human is foreign; people planned according to an efficient scheme, as one plans machines; people whom the inhibitions of a moral consciousness and a spiritual personality have been trained out of; people for whom every reference to a transcendent authority has become meaningless; animals living without future and without hope in the moment alone, and planned for it, as muscle and nerve.

Such training pursues the mystery of iniquity to the very deepest roots of human origins. These people are enticed into "missteps," perversions, violations of civil law, into fraud, theft, outrage. This is done in order to get a blackmailer's hold on them, and thrust them upon the road of amorality, along which they are then pursued to the point of utter unscrupulousness. The qualities of pride and license are awakened in them. They are allowed a chance to display themselves as the "masters," to use their instincts of cruelty, greed for power, and arrogance.

No corrective can exist at the same time with such training of the younger generation. The family, the most powerful cell for the domestication of man, is systematically destroyed. With wily acuteness they attack the point that is at once the most powerful and the most delicate and sensitive spot in humanity. The cells of the private sphere are not destroyed for political reasons alone. The war is on against the foundations of civilization, the primitive beginnings of domestication, against the cells of authority, of subordination, of self-control, of suppression of blind instincts, against the whole elemental nature of human education. Let

198

man lose all ties! Let him become part of the masses, and, as masses, capable of being collectivized. Let him have no responsibilities toward anything except the public power. Let him tame his instincts only when it seems useful to this power. If his lusts are incestuous or parricidal, so much the better, let him satisfy them. It is desired to have people free of the Oedipus complex, free of the weight of civilization.

Release of all sub-human instincts, sexual freedom, total promiscuity with untroubled conscience — such are the rewards of strict training in the service of Leviathan, such the compensations for total unfreedom in the domain of a former political and social life. This release is the opposite of discipline. Hitler orders restraints flung away, thus fulfilling the secret yearnings of a large part of this generation, which is infected with dislike of civilization, and is going roaming back into the desert that beckons further on, the promised land.

THE UNMASKING OF LEVIATHAN

Casting off restraints is the ultimate consummation of the "process of intellectual emancipation." It is logical; what else counts? Socialism in its popular form, after having traced back all intellectual values to material conditions and movements, still demands an altruistic attitude. How so, what for? Is it not much more consistent in that case to toss everything overboard, and is not this the secret of Hitler's success, particularly with the younger generation? He has told boys and girls to "enjoy their youth," but he has also told the young men to kill and torture their outlawed adversaries, told them to rob and burn, told them to oppress defenseless Jews. Surely this is a general application of an attitude prepared, nay glorified, among part of the proletariat by the intellectuals — the ruthless struggle against the bourgeoisie. And once again has not Hitler simply drawn the final conclusion? The man who will submit to slavery deserves to be a slave. There is no such thing as a living soul, so why not shoot and trample down what is useless? Even Nietzsche advised that what was falling ought to be pushed.

Fling off restraints, stand up, a free man! Man? To be human may perhaps mean to interpose restraints. Human no more, then? Hitler and his people have no inhibitions; hence their rapidity, hence the surprises, and incredible feats. He's just playing Indian, people said of his policies — Fenimore Cooper in politics. This is incorrect. It is absence of restraints, complete lack of misgivings or rules of the game. The Neanderthal man has broken the thin crust of humanity, as someone very aptly wrote recently. If we are going to think in race categories, why not some such comparison? The Neanderthal man is he to whom civilization, created by higher beings and forced upon him, is the very essence of the hateful.

How does all this differ from the things more shrewd and knowing people have long done in secret? The wiser and more knowing ones who did it for private pleasure, not as a principle, not as a general rule, but as a privilege of select free spirits? But like everything else this attitude succumbs to the tendency of all products of civilization to decline. It becomes commonplace, it is debased, it winds up in the gutter.

Do we understand the aversion and yet the hidden sympathies

of all these "free spirits" for Hitler? The secret admiration? He has simply done a masterly job, and is a "great man." Is it not remarkable how much sympathy, how much loving hatred Hitler enjoys precisely among that particular sort of liberals who raved about "living dangerously" long before Goebbels, and considered themselves men of the Renaissance because they deceived their wives with waitresses?

National Socialism is the most wily and consistent attempt in world history to render the evil in man and the evil man politically useful. In all countries there are people who find pleasure in torture, enjoy brutality, and are ready for any cruelty. These people, hitherto held in check by the rules of society, by fear of the penal laws or by a civil order that gives them no chance to live according to their instincts, are lured from their dark corners by the new gospel of force, the will to power and unrestraint. Honor beckons, they are enticed by promotion and every enjoyment for their particular requirements.

Something resembling a world conspiracy of all the criminal instincts and forces in man is now arising. As gangsters, members of the demi-monde and criminals recognize one another at a glance, so today there is a great International of the criminal world turned political. We are perhaps only at the beginning of a monstrous development. Whither it may lead and with what it may threaten the civilized world, no man can predict.

In comparison with the other totalitarian regimes National Socialism is the one really dangerous enemy of human society. The attempt to realize Communism makes use of an absolutist power machinery, but it is itself in line with the European ideas of human progress and liberating enlightenment and thus still belongs to the tradition of the Western European mind. Continuing to develop the doctrine of Socialism, it is the legitimate and perhaps last successor to a process of secularization and revolution that has gone on throughout the last four hundred years. Along with this Western development it may be beyond such a process; it may change; it is alive with the creative impulses of our civilization, with all the possibilities of regeneration and adaptation. National Socialism, on the other hand, is "the other" — complete nothingness, the absolute negation of the Western World, of civilization. It cannot go backward, and it cannot go forward beyond itself; it is only itself. It is dangerous because it does more than give opportunity for a tremendous rise of those elements in all countries that are uprooted, unoccupied, dispossessed, under-privileged and full of envy and resentment, and have therefore lost all civil and moral restraints. In addition there are all those who want security at any price, who are solicitous for the positions they have achieved, and fear nothing but having to return to unemployment, privation, and social ostracism. The world is full of creatures on every level of society who are ready to pay any price so long as they need not abandon their profitable positions. Faithful to the program recorded in its book, National Socialism appeals to the lowest instincts of mankind. It did so on a small scale in the "fight for power," as it does today on a large scale. It thus altogether dissolves the shattered old order. From the masses produced by this disintegration it forms its own order, with the base instincts as the cement of the community and the element of union. Can such a thing last and endure?

It presents the danger of a permanent Fall of Man. A new picture of mankind is pushing toward realization — the human termite. Here is the metaphysically truly iniquitous assault on a humanity that once recognized itself as the image of God. The termite state is the real meaning of Leviathan. In it God is cheated out of his creation. The spark of human individualism is extinguished.

But is one not forced into the same path by all the future Utopias that propose to surrender personality for the sake of collectivism, liberty for the sake of Utopian equality, and the creative force for the sake of uniformity? Perhaps these ideas can be pursued further. The termite state comes into being through the destruction of mass sexuality. And indeed behind the enlightened sexual morality, behind the transformation of sex from a myth to a hygienic requirement (as rationalist socialism of every origin has long placarded it, and as National Socialism has now taken it over), there is indeed something much like a destruction of sexuality. It is denatured, canalized, becomes unimportant, and ceases to be a factor of turbulence. In the opinion of the socialists a good share of irrationality is thus rationalized; in the opinion of the National Socialists man is thus prepared to yield to coercion in another field. The same is true of another urge, the property instinct, the individual acquisitive instinct. In this light, is popular socialism a suitable adversary for National Socialism — is it not a secret ally? From that standpoint, yes! For does it not lead to a new, base destruction of man?

It is National Socialism that unmasks the true character of Leviathan. Can the Leviathan, therefore, continue to be the source of help and information for other political forces? Can it become the wish-image of the future order, no matter in what incarnation or disguise — as a state for the social functions, as a new democracy or an authoritarian state? Coercive training, the "planning" of human beings, of younger generations, and the whole tendency toward machinery, toward deliberate guidance, the whole pattern of uniformity, collectivization, depersonalization, coercion, regulation: is not all this rendered impossible by the unmasking of Leviathan as the pseudo order founded exclusively on power, subjugation, and obedience, robbing men of their essential spirit? Is it still possible to "plan" categories of men after this exposure of rationalism with its "despotism of reason"? The great process of unmasking all the ideologies, which constituted the intellectual history of the nineteenth century, finds its termination and dialectical reversal in the revelation that a rationalistic, totally mundane human order is impossible because it can exist only as a coercive order, and thus leads to absolutism, where it becomes the total negation of man and his civilization.

If we were to put this statement into mythical language, we could say, It is the mystery of iniquity that has given National Socialism its appearance of power. And it is also this mystery that is the essence of Leviathan.

Leviathan remains the *deus mortalis,* the mortal god. He bestows his order by cheating man of his nature, whether one call it immortality, the soul, personality, no matter what.

I see a rising flood of hopelessness, of despair at the impotence of good will; it is the very opposite of the unbounded optimism of the old liberals. No, surely reason has not been victorious.

But is that any excuse for the thoughtful people to become nihilists now too? Nihilism is something that we shall never vanquish; perhaps it is only the new form of evil. The "engineer of the universe," indeed, we shall have to cast off. He is in the shape of Leviathan, the form that the dominion of nihilism takes.

THE WORLD SOVEREIGNTY OF NIHILISM

Hitler once spoke of his "Copernican" deed in giving a new center to the universe. What is this center that stands still, and what is it that moves instead of being static, as we formerly imagined it to be? What is this Copernican achievement — power instead of liberty, race instead of equality?

Only the narrow minded or those who will not see can deny that there is something majestic about Hitler's plans and ideas. If it were not for this factor, opening the view beyond narrow European concepts, how would it have been possible for so many intelligent people to fall under his spell? Despite all his vileness there is about Hitler's undertakings a freedom from preconceived ideas that in a way is a positive release. His lack of restraint and his emancipation from "recognized opinions and judgments" have enabled the man to see the critical points of our life more impartially than we have done, especially we so-called educated people. There really is some truth in the statement that he has been able to see through sham greatness, and reduce it to its true proportions — just as he perceived important outlines of the new reality before we others would admit it to be true.

If ability to see through things and reduce complication to a simple nucleus constitutes greatness of a sort, one cannot altogether deny it to Hitler. No more can we say he lacks another quality likewise considered a sign of political stature, namely the ability to instill intuition into other gifted persons, and make them work for his own purposes. Evidently some fluid emanates from the man, giving strength and exaltation; so hardened a skeptic as President Schacht of the Reichsbank has said more than once that he comes out from each audience with Hitler refreshed and invigorated. This is not a mere neo-Byzantine manner of speaking; it is an impression that many people have reported to me. For my part Hitler never gave me this feeling, but there was another that I could never resist — the widening of the horizon. Hitler tears down the barriers of every man's cosmogony, and shows him "the kingdoms of the world, and the glory of them."

I use the words of the Gospel deliberately. It is the daemonic part of the man, this gift of showing problems in a new light and opening new expanses of horizon, that gives him his influence. We cannot conquer these daemonic temptations and the forces they embody unless we look them impartially in the eye, and find out on what their attraction is based. The fear that Hitler may shortly manoeuver democracy into an untenable situation in the political war is not unfounded. For instance he may oblige democracy to stand up openly for what is antiquated and backward, and to turn against sensible progress. It may have to fight for a Europe that no one wants restored — a Europe cut up by frontiers, by national dissensions, by economic protectionism, filled with "obstacles to traffic" of every sort, a pre-war, pre-revolutionary Europe. Or it may have to fight for a domestic political order that possibly still interests a small elite, but has lost all attraction for the masses, who can no longer become excited about principles and political debates. Or it may be a social order in which the class-struggle idea, which scarcely has any real meaning left for the workers, is propagated on the one side, while on the other side social and economic privileges now devoid of all significance are defended. Or it may be necessary to take up the cudgels for an economic structure that has long since lost its essential characteristics, but is defending all the more violently its outlying fringes — an orthodox currency system, an outworn commercial organization, an antiquated financial policy, and the like.

Suppose Hitler really does "lead" Europe with a moderate, perhaps self-restricted authority, instead of dominating it? Suppose after all he were to adopt moderation, and draw up conditions of peace that would concede the members of his federation or his European league intelligently defined liberties along with the benefits of a great economic and administrative unit? That is, what if this continent under National Socialist leadership should take on the form toward which its historical development has long been tending: an economic and political unit that would not fritter away the greater part of its energies in overcoming the difficulties and barriers that it keeps creating for itself? A unit in which the diversity and multiplicity of inhabitants as nations, peoples and stocks would be left intact, encouraged, and even developed wherever appropriate, in regional self-government, in the cultivation of civilization, custom, intellectual character? What if the result were to be something like the much-heralded United States of Europe? Not in the mechanical and rationalistically stereotyped fashion that has been the aim of all Pan-Europeans so far, but in a way adapted to the character of Europe, individually suited to the actual conditions, to the continuing forces of tradition and historic development? An order, that is, which would make its arrangements for each case — arrangements for Holland different from those for Norway, for Switzerland different from those for Poland, etc. — not everything on one pattern, not according to the efficient program that is the joy of the radical planners? Suppose Europe were to be a unit in which the whole rich historical background of peoples and stocks on the most various levels of civilization were preserved and cultivated?

What then?

Will it then be said in the democracies, will it be said in Great Britain, where the substance of Western European civilization is preserved in its purest form, that the battle is being fought for the restoration of the old Europe, for all the national democracies with their economic protection, their domestic aggression against stocks and peoples that do not belong to the "national state"? For the establishment of new, definite frontiers, which will be the just ones; although no such frontiers can possibly exist in Central and Eastern Europe? For a league of nations that will continue to be impotent, for a disarmament that will be sabotaged, for a collective security that will remain a phantom? All for an *"il faut en finir,"* for retribution, for final destruction of a Pan-German, Greater Prussian militarism that is no longer a reality, because it is now submerged in the far more dangerous aggressiveness of the new Jacobinism?

To discuss proclamations, programs, peace, or war aims is to waste time. It tempts one to believe something can be accomplished in that way, whereas reality advances in another direction, while a new reality has already come into being, and is establishing itself with all the momentum of actuality in the face of programs and plans.

This reality tempts not only the masses but the people of intelligence, not only the German people but the subject nations. It deludes them into resignation — to say nothing of the political jobbers who see their golden opportunity in the present situation. Lethargy and despondency are beginning to grow rank in Germany and the occupied territories. Despite all privations and humiliations there is a predominant idea that with the present German regime at least you know where you are, whereas no one can tell whether a new dispensation would be any better. People are beginning to reconcile themselves to the idea that at least National Socialism pursues the line of a new Europe with a unified economic structure. Once the war is over, people console themselves, the real building-up will begin, and all those who share in it, even those now politically oppressed, will profit. Our Forty-Eighters' dream of German unity and democracy was realized by Bismarck in his own way, with blood and iron. Might the dream of the Pan-Europeans, in turn, become a fact in Hitler's own way, with blood and iron?

But what more is this than a mere sham solution, promising the same opportunity as the true solution? It discredits and renders impossible the motives and energies of the true solution, forestalls it, and builds up out of correct premises and justified requirements a grave obstacle to the life and future of the Western World.

209

We must not believe for a moment in the reality of such a moderate peace solution by Hitler, leading to a sort of saturation of the nineteenth-century European nationalist and socialist revolutionary tendencies. What we *must* believe in, on the other hand, is the fact that the masses in the democracies, and not they alone, can be and are being deluded into belief in such a realization through peace with National Socialist Germany. For these masses, and not they alone, are eager to be done at last with the age of nineteenth-century nationalist revolution. They are as weary of the everlasting boundary disputes over national aspirations as of the class struggle, elevated into a myth by socialist theories. By their unwillingness to see this fact, present-day statesmen are depriving themselves of a decisive resource for leadership.

As a transition, an intermediate phase, in order to cause the struggle to be interrupted by political means, Hitler's European order is a temptation against which inoculation is necessary.

It is worth while to keep pointing out an idea deeply rooted in National Socialist circles, namely that in all probability Germany's world domination cannot be attained at one bound, but that even a third attempt will be necessary. The truce from 1918 to 1933 represented no loss to Germany. It offered just the necessary opportunity to discipline the German nation and bring about an entirely new constellation of forces in foreign affairs. The National Socialist elite have hoped for something similar from a second intervening quasi-armistice. These ideas also have some reference to Bismarck's achievement of national unity in the nineteenth century, so skillfully accomplished through three different wars. They are even fond of going back still further and speaking of a third Punic War, in which British Carthage will be finally annihilated.

The slightest reflection will show that an interruption of war by a compromise peace must inevitably mean Hitler's ultimate victory. Another start would enable him to destroy Russia and England singly, to make use of the experiences of the war thus far, and to fill the gaps in his armament. We can already detect Hitler shuffling the card of a new peaceful interval into the pack, and can see how the card is to be played. If Hitler succeeds, not even in making peace, but only in preventing a synchronization of two wars, east and west, against him, then the true visage of his demands for European sovereignty and the basic lines of his world regime will come more clearly into the open. He cannot stop once he has started along this road. An absolute maximum of power and sovereignty is a *sine qua non* of his subsistence in power in Europe, and even in Germany. No matter what may be broadcast about his future moderation and his desire to undo the actions that he recognizes as mistakes, we must not be deceived about the fact that Hitler is bound to speculate craftily upon his chances of getting by political warfare what he cannot get by force of arms. For that matter, we may remember the situation when Hitler came into power in Germany. Outwardly his movement was on the point of collapse. His situation was desperate; but for that very reason there were groups in Germany who regarded National Socialism as ripe for negotiation, pliable enough in its distress to be useful for their purposes. I am repeating myself here, but I do not think I can say often enough that this turn of events, which brought Hitler into power in the most desperate crisis of his career, indelibly stamped his thinking, and inspired him to a new gamble with high stakes, this time in the arena of world affairs.

The moment we reflect that a European order by itself cannot exist at all, it becomes evident that anything as yet known of Hitler's new European order is no more than an expedient of the political war. Even if a unified economic and political order on the Continent can be achieved, even if it does not mean the concentration, described earlier, of all the instruments of power in great monopolies controlled by Germany alone, still such a European order will be insufficient to assure a new state of peace. At best the National Socialist order would transfer existing nationalist state rivalries from a European scale to a world scale, and thus inevitably cause new complications of universal import — to say nothing of the fact that Europe is not self-sufficient and therefore is subject to new expansionist urges. The interplay and counterplay of "major areas" can do nothing to secure peace, but will merely offer new scope for a final clash of powers over world hegemony.

A new balance on a world scale guaranteed by Hitler and Mussolini, perhaps by Japan and Stalin as well, is chimerical. It would be no more real with the advent even of Great Britain and the United States. British Empire, Hitler's Europe, Russia's Pan-Asiatic Union, Pan-America — among these there will never be a real balance. It is merely the starting point for a decision upon world sovereignty. The necessity for concentrating the instruments of world power would very soon lead not only to the elimination of all bypaths and secondary focal points (such as Italian aspirations) within the major areas, but would bring about the elimination of the competing powers. If the demand for concentration and centralization of power is yielded to, we cannot suddenly turn around and follow the opposite principles of respect for others, diversity of power nuclei, rivalry.

Balance belongs to the vocabulary of an altogether different political order, namely the opposing, British-Anglo-Saxon order. A system which unites the states that have grown historically from Europe cannot be established by subjugating some of these nations, but only through the general interest of all. And only a Europe ordered in this fashion, in turn, is capable of entering into a similar but more extensive community of continents. An order in which centralized and totalitarian major areas direct the democratic major areas means not a termination, but a mere phase within the great revolution.

TRISTITIA SAECULI

This process of destruction, concealed by intellectual makeshifts, began as the proud emancipation of human society from the rubbish of the past and the dreams of its childhood. Its end is absolute nothingness, the individual's clear consciousness or dull fear of belonging to today alone. You snatch as much pleasure and power as possible in this one life, in order at last to surrender — drugging your fear cynically and coldly with a jest, or hysterically, as the case may be — to complete extinction in the nothingness of death. Human lives have lost all value.

It is *tristitia saeculi,* the melancholy of the world, that confronts the "divine melancholy." This means that one no longer claims to be a child of God. People want to be relieved from the demands of a higher humanity, relieved of intellectual exertion and moral decisions. People want to vegetate in a state of abstraction where the substitute for security consists in the absence of fear and hope.

But in an age when every kind of faith has become ridiculous and impossible, how can a political community exist without a common view of life professed by everyone? Must not the anxious patriot hoping to save his people, as well as the unscrupulous power-seeker, resort to the one expedient still remaining to hold together something like a community — coercion, enforced belief?

All the questions center in one question: how is faith still possible in this age? For the majority of all human beings the question is already: what can be put in place of a dead faith in order to escape from the chaos? This is a question of burning importance not simply for Germany, possibly France, and the European Continent. England too, the Anglo-Saxon world, is living only on the sublimated remnant of a Christian belief that has long since begun to evaporate. What today is still a convention might vanish as completely as in Germany for the present younger generation. The process of ideological deflation has not been carried through to its conclusion here as it has on the Continent; but can it be halted?

This is the gravest doubt that exists in respect to the possibility of regenerating our Western world.

In certain orgies of the great French Revolution, it was at least the Goddess of Reason who was put upon the throne, even though she might be represented by a naked woman. The despotism was at any rate, as Robespierre said, the despotism of reason. But what is set on the throne in Germany is Caliban, the human creature sunk lower than the beasts, and without consciousness of a higher vocation, or any desire for it.

People disdain all higher humanity, and enjoy the vandal feeling of having destroyed the temple within themselves. How indeed could the message of Christianity find hearers now — Christianity, which sets up as a requirement for grace the consciousness of sin and of the necessity for a conversion that even the clergyman today balks at calling penance lest he lose the last remnants of a congregation of so-called believers?

And yet it's precisely the utter meaninglessness and worthlessness of this de-Christianized, godless life that should bring people back to the roots of Christianity. This was the very point that everything depended on, as the revolutionaries in Dostoievsky's uncanny forecast of our European nihilism pointed out: No crystal palace in this life, no past order gives any assurance of humanity. What counts is belief in the transcendence of the human essence — let us say it simply as Dostoievsky himself says it — whether there is an immortality or not.

But what Dostoievsky did not yet see was that man, uprooted by the technological revolution, and living in a constant state of narcosis, not only *can* no longer believe but does not *want* to believe. This is the condition that the old church fathers called *acedia,* sloth. It is the sloth unwilling any longer to assume the obligations implied by the higher destiny of man. It is the sloth that grows from the melancholy of the world, or, in modern words, it is the negation of any higher self in man.

It may be regarded as bad taste to mingle religious sentiments with political discussion. And yet without this religious crisis our whole fate is quite incomprehensible. Finding one's way to such insights is a long process, particularly for the man who has felt that he must stick to externals. The two great questions of destiny remain unanswered: How can we bring home to a people, a younger generation, that which not merely leaves them cold, but does not even touch them at all? If the survival of our civilization depends on a reawakening of the Christian faith, is civilization not dead already, with us simply playing the part of hosts at the wake?

Is it possible for a person to be a Christian at all any more — is it possible for a whole people, a state, a society? Are not the only remaining Christians the pious in the land, the stragglers, the underprivileged or the aging, the sickly, we who are already on the downward slope in life?

What is Christianity, anyway — what is its nature? Is it simply a "sense of dependence as such," dependence on some faith, some "destiny"? As Hitler speaks of it, it is something like the "good and the beautiful." Is it Pantheism, Deism perhaps, a scrap of hope that possibly this animal existence may not be quite the end of it after all? Can religion still exist in this age? Is it not simply a "petrification" of an alien state of consciousness, projecting into the present from vanished ages? Are we not already much further along than one could guess even from atheist propaganda or from all the attempts at a neopaganism that is doing no more than batter down open doors? Are we not in a post-Christian age to which even "doubt has become suspect"? The present genera-

216

distinction to power and gain, but not in "accommodation to state and mundane things." The "artificial replanting of Christianity for purposes of good behavior" he regards as futile.

It is true that all intended efforts at a renaissance of Christianity are subject to an implacable tribunal. Good will and the intention to believe are not enough. A "planned" Christian Action such as would seem necessary to us for a regeneration of the Western world would be the most insipid, senseless and destructive undertaking among all the planning enterprises that occupy so many of our contemporaries. It will fail because influences outside faith itself — maintenance of a social order, the restoration of orderly functioning in the state, an ethical basis for civilization — do not really lead to faith, but only to a belief that faith is necessary. "Men often take their imagination for their heart," says Pascal, "and they think they are converts as soon as they begin to think about becoming converted." Merely to realize the necessity of conversion is not Christianity.

The difficulty of re-Christianization lies not alone in the present outer estrangement from anything transcendent, but also in the eternal paradox of faith, which has always been that wishes and good will by themselves are not enough — least of all the wish that would use faith as a means toward order in the secular community.

It was not without hidden meaning that Hobbes took the name of the beast of the Apocalypse for his *deus mortalis* and for the temptation toward a purely mundane human order rooted altogether in earthly things. He fully realized the "presumption," religiously speaking, of such an order. He knew he was setting up a structure consistently opposite to the Christian order — an anti-Christian order. He knew, too, that basically this order of his could be combated only by the Christian spiritual order, and not within its own sphere. In that sphere his order is unassailable, logical, conclusive, and deceptively attractive; anyone who allows himself to be touched by this god of Hobbes' falls into his clutches like the wayward soul who once made a pact with the Evil One.

If the dominion of Leviathan can fundamentally be overthrown only by religious forces, then it appears to be now unshakable, and the day of final realization seems at hand — the kingdom of Anti-christ. How can the Christian order, whose secular incarnation has already become weak and wavering, summon the strength to conquer outside its own spiritual sphere?

Perhaps, after all, during these past years something new has touched us — something new to *us,* but actually forever old. We have learned the reality of evil, the metaphysical power and effect of evil. This Leviathan is evil. In the Gospel sense it is the tempter, promising all the kingdoms of the world and the glory of them if only one will fall down and worship. It is the evil whose strength and violence we have realized through the dissension and torments of these past years. It is not human evil, no petty every-day baseness, but the power, the quite admirable force of magnificent evil, which has enchanted the great artists of the ages even more potently than sacred things have done. It is the daemonic evil that shares in the intellectual sphere and the creative powers of the demiurge.

From this experience of evil a path may open to the experience of the faith in which evil is vanquished.

values. The Jewish mind, which in order to attain equal civil rights had torn itself loose from the strongest of bonds, from the old, venerable authority that governed every aspect of life, became the model and the example of what utter absence of authority man might dare aspire to. In an age when people were consciously seeking restraints and authority, therefore, there were also bound to be honest motives for combating the most prominent representative of the struggle for emancipation, at the same time that one fought against dissolution and for a new authority.

When the movement of ideological deflation reached its logical conclusion and reversed itself, once again Jews were the leaders who called most audibly for a return from freedom to a new absolutism. "It is not liberation and development of the ego that are the secret and the commandment of the age. What it needs, what it demands, what it will get, is — terrorism." Thus Thomas Mann, with the acute sensitivity to changes in the human mind that this great artist always displays, makes his revolutionist, Naphta, speak before the first World War. "It is an uncharitable misunderstanding of the younger generation to suppose they find their enjoyment in freedom. Their deepest delight is in obedience." This was the desperate situation in which the dialectics of the Western European mind had involved us, the younger generation of the last war; Mann portrayed the hopelessness of it in his great picture of *The Magic Mountain*. Here too he predicted the coming development. It was the acute dialectic intelligence of the Jew that had helped create the situation. Here the liberty to which he owed his political and social equality reversed itself, becoming thraldom and terrorism. The paradox is that the Jew

225

himself helped to drown out the "summons to Sinai."

The whole domain of anti-Semitism is paradoxical. This is so because it is not merely a phenomenon of political and social life or of a special historical situation, but has its roots on the transcendental level. Even the special rubber stamps used on the passports of the Jews in Germany indicate the metaphysical fact that Israel is being persecuted as God's chosen people. This is not "the civil war of a majority against a minority," and consequently also not a mere "national calamity," as Mommsen put it. Nor can anti-Semitism be terminated simply by restoration of equality in the eyes of the law, or protection "as well against open infraction of law as against administrative fraud." Greater exertions than this are needed. For the Christian there can be no anti-Semitism. For him the Jews even today are the chosen people, who will find the end of their sufferings and wanderings in complete restoration of their special character as the chosen. The Christian faith has always begun to disintegrate whenever anyone has tried, as for instance Marcion did, to separate the Old Testament from the New. But what does this attitude of the Christian mean to the present day? For more than fifteen centuries the Christian faith has gone hand in hand with pogroms and the ghetto; only the great humanitarian revolution gave civil equality to the Jews and put an end to the ghetto. Is it not, therefore, synonymous with a new ghetto when that revolution is attacked, and this from motives of Christianity? Is it not simply logical, then, that anti-Semitism has also become a political demand?

Consequently the destiny of Judaism will always be on the side of revolution, of liberation, of dissolution.

But this conflicts with its true intellectual vocation, which is to remain on the side of law, conservation, tradition, upon the great historical road to a higher humanity. Only the Jews alone can extricate themselves from this tragic bewilderment. No gentile can help. He can only respect the conflict, and expect the Jews to master it successfully. For Judaism is the strongest of the conservative forces. It is the oldest root of our Western tradition. In fact Judaism, along with Hellenic civilization and Christianity, is the imperishable substance of our Christian Occident, the eternal "summons to Sinai," against which man keeps forever rebelling.

This tragic confusion puts upon the Jew, most conspicuously among all men, the burden of a never-ending battle. It is the perpetual contrast between revolution and tradition, between liberation and bondage. Each is a vocation and a human destiny, though not always equally so. Because he, of all men, suffers most from this contrast, the Jew is in danger of being made responsible for this insoluble conflict. The impossible task of being human is what crude men rebel against through anti-Semitism.

8

The "Finest Hour"

You no longer count the days of the bombing, nor the weeks. You get used to this new life, its ebb and flow, its pulse and breathing, the fiercer attacks and the weaker ones. Many people you knew, whom you met but a few days ago, are among the victims today; houses that yesterday you saw teeming with life today are ruined. There is the shop where you used to get milk; it is demolished; the girl who used to bring it is among the dead. The vegetable woman is in the hospital, gravely injured. The tailor's shop has been hit by a bomb. Yonder the delicate, ethereal French nuns were killed. There were six of them; two were keeping the night vigil, and they were saved. What have this little street and these little shops, destroyed during the mid-morning shopping hour, to do with Hitler's dominion over the air? The nights are longer, the days more gloomy. Bombs suddenly drop from the clouds, and whether you are riding in a taxi or a bus, or working at the office, sitting at your desk, suddenly there is this roar, near or far.

But life is the thing that comes first in this immense city. Employees arrive punctually at offices and shops, and the armies of workmen fight the invisible battles of the war. The havoc disappears, the ruins are cleared away, people prepare for further trials. Patience, self-control, moderation will not be lost. And some day these people will come up out of the shelters and basements, and the other, the new, the yet more difficult work will begin: peace.

The decisive importance of these weeks stands out more and more plainly. A battle has been fought, and we have seen only the smallest part of it. It is the great and as yet nameless battle that may already have determined the future course of the war. What has been said about the finest hour and the great accomplishment of so small a minority may be true, and more than that. It may be England's privilege to reconcile tradition and revolution for a long time to come.

I stand in Trafalgar Square, where there are now two deep bomb craters, and watch an exciting air battle going on over our heads. You see the white smoke pennants of a German squadron flying in close formation. Three British battle planes circle around them. The strangest spirals and figures are traced against the sky. Clouds slide in front of the spectacle. The battle goes on, invisible to us — a battle of spirits.

The spiritual battle too needs its "finest hour," just as the battle for the future of Europe does.

"Now first, Sir, permit me to observe that the use of force alone is but temporary. It may subdue for a moment; but it does not remove the necessity of subduing again; and a nation is not governed which is perpetually to be conquered." These words of

230

Burke's were spoken about the American states at one of the most critical periods of British history. This is the second time that absolutism, after running through the whole continent of Europe, has been halted by the Anglo-Saxon world. Hobbes, who wrote his doctrine of the Leviathan here, found the reality in the French and Prussian states. The influences that prevented England from going the way of the Continent are the same that give her today her mission of opposing the new absolutism.

There is the entity of a tradition never yet broken. There are the historical forces that have so far been strong enough to resist the temptations of doctrinarianism. There is the independence that has asserted itself in oppositon to every political or intellectual absolutism. There is the firm distinction between the spheres of public and private life — not mere theory, but a corrective influence, organically connected with practical life, against the absolutist tendencies that always strive to dominate public life. There is a true democracy sprung from corporate bodies and an attitude of personal independence; it differs fundamentally from all the intellectual forms of democracy, built on theories and doctrines. It is the irrationality of this democratic life that makes it strong — the irrationality inherent in the individual sense of personal independence and in the religious roots of personal responsibility.

These forces have produced, in the United States, a commonwealth that has preserved and developed in tune with the times its indpendence, the political principles of its liberty, despite a good many features of hyper-efficiency. The British colonial empire has given birth, after many aberrations and setbacks, to a form of free leadership and trustee administration for great areas and heterogeneous peoples, such as has never existed before in history.

Thus we have a power group that appears closely united by origin, history, political traditions and libertarian leadership, and seems destined to extend the principle of trustee administration beyond its existing sphere of influence to the formation of an inclusive world order.

A development such as this cannot be systematically anticipated. It must come into existence as a fact. The whole plan for a new order and the defeat of the modern Leviathan does indeed depend to this extent on historical occurrences, which come about not because they have been rationally planned but because they are based on actual historical conditions. Unless there is a power nucleus for a rising new order, any abstract, rational plan for a European or world union is doomed to remain a political theory. Economic and political planning based on purely rational considerations, and going along beside actual events, contains the threat of confusion, and diversion from what is concretely possible toward Utopian experiments that are bound either to fail, or to involve us in the temptations and bewilderments of the present age. The new order cannot be made; it must grow from and with the requirements of war and reconstruction. This can be done only piecemeal. That is to say, we cannot begin by setting up a fixed optimum plan for the building of a new order. On the contrary its realization will depend, in detail and in the large, on the actual conditions taken as a starting-point — i.e., the existing reality of the Empire and the American Union — and on the positive course of events in other fields.

232

It is part of the great English tradition to follow exactly the political course that is now necessary if we are to escape the enticement of the new absolutism. The temptation becomes inescapable the moment one starts from an abstract point, and gives rationalist and doctrinaire notions preference over the historical realities. There is no choice but to start from what now exists, and to use the proved principles, developed within the government of the Empire, as constituent elements of a still greater and more universal order. No European union, no scheme, it matters not how wonderful, for a United States of Europe can possibly replace the substantial nucleus of power and development (perhaps already growing up) that would become a reality through close cooperation of the Empire with the United States.

But such a connection, if it should become a fact, must not in turn lead to a sort of Utopian super-state such as many people seem to be thinking of. Instead it must preserve all the existing variety of form, individuality, and special rights. To promote centralization and uniformity, rather than the national state, in a sort of international state superstructure, cannot accord with the living tradition of the two great Anglo-Saxon commonwealths, which have successfully resisted such sproutings of modern absolutism at home. Any extended order that might form around the Atlantic nucleus would have to take account of the needs and differences of the peoples, rather than proceeding according to a uniform plan, and breaking historical forms in order to follow a scheme that was rationally more satisfactory.

The tyranny of the totalitarian states cannot be overcome by making modern absolutism the tool of an international socialism or of rationalistic planning ideas, instead of the instrument of a nationalist imperialism. The temptation to construct on paper is strong, because the goal of rationally convincing political and economic planning is popular and, in a way, attractive, whereas by comparison the outlines of such a world commonwealth as might grow up around the British Empire and the United States will seem a jumbled compromise, ill thought out and unsatisfactory in the light of reason.

All rational thinkers feel affronted by "traditional rubbish" and the demands of historical accumulation. Like the French tragedy, they demand the unities of time, place and action. They demand the concentration of power and the centralization of the executive. They could not possibly regard an intention to avoid just this concentration and centralization as anything but immaturity of judgment and failure to rise above a puerile level. Once again we see the sole vocation of the Anglo-Saxon world, as shown by the fact that it regards historical events as a more decisive power than "the despotism of reason," to quote Robespierre again. It avoids the unity of power and the centralization demanded by logic, and instead, by an actual and not merely theoretical separation of powers, maintains something like a plural community — the only possible form for any future world union or federation.

This would mean that special forms of legal self-administration must be developed within the super-national economic order and the super-national regulation of the social functions. Economic and social planning is necessary in such matters as labor supply, settlement, etc.; it must not be allowed to become the task of a centralized super-state machine, and thus the starting point for a growing, centralized power machinery. In the same way the existing tendency toward centralization should be politically combated as far as possible by favoring separate entities wherever history and geography have produced them, and thus furthering political decentralization. Decentralization would be cultivated in all matters not directly concerning foreign affairs, the army, and a common law.

The British Empire and the United States alone are destined to assume the leadership and trusteeship in forming such an order, because they alone fulfill two requirements: they do not construct geometrically, but suit their institutions to the demands of reality, because they have the courage to make mistakes and to correct them; and they have developed a libertarian leadership that never uses the persons being led as tools, but only as creatures of their own free will and their own responsibility.

Other nations too have had a similar vocation for leadership. Many possible developments toward new forms of free federal commonwealth can be imagined. The Germans too had the vocation. Perhaps we were the first to be called on the European continent. But we made wrong use of the experiences of the First World War, which definitely limited our will to dominate, and might have set us upon the only possible path to permanent recovery. We repeated the mistake that had wrecked us before. A few of the younger conservative element saw the part that we might have taken in a new order in Europe. They rightly recognized the causes of "Europa irredenta," and they saw the only possible ways to overcome the national democratic dissension of

235

Europe. They saw Germany's mission as leadership, not domination, of the Central and Eastern European nations that shared in the common misfortune of dividing frontiers and small, artificial areas. These elements were politically powerless. Their ideas and personalities were usurped, misused and corrupted by National Socialism.

Thus Germany tossed away the greatest opportunity she ever had in her history, in exchange for the chimera of world dominion and power madness. No nation can take the place of another and assume its mission. Just as our false decision rendered impossible a German share in the great achievement, another achievement — the union of Great Britain and France offered by Churchill just before the French collapse — has become impossible as a backbone for the future order. It is the personal decisions of nations and individual leaders that set the future world scene, not the intellectual projections of committees and scientific experts.

One thing, however, is irrevocable even now. The concept of the "Western world" as Europe, and of Europe as a unit, is no longer valid. The transformation of reality is not only in the direction of greater economic expanses but in the direction of true planetary universality. This is a painful process of transformation, which does away with the political, intellectual, and economic claims of Europe to dominance.

THE BIRD FIGHTS ITS WAY OUT OF THE SHELL

This Second World War has come upon Europe like a judge's sentence without appeal. The European continent is ceasing to be the intellectual and political center that it has been for so long.

The center of gravity is shifting westward. Around the Atlantic Ocean some sort of new Empire of peace may grow up. The power nucleus of the new order is springing from a union of the Anglo-Saxon peoples. Europe will become a hinterland. The MENE MENE TEKEL of National Socialism predicting the end of Europe may become a reality, but not as the prophets have interpreted it. As the great states of Asia Minor, the empires of the old world along the Euphrates, the Tigris and the Nile fell back before the Mediterranean world, so apparently it is our fate to sink to second or third rank.

It was not fated so. Another course of events would have been possible. A second chance was given us; we did not use it. We misused it. No European order, no matter how rationally designed, can prevent the new reality of an Atlantic world center from growing up during the present war, or stop the creation of an order with gradations that no theories can get rid of. Nor should anyone want to get rid of them.

For if any new order can come into being at all through this great revolution it will develop according to the requirements of actual needs and urgent necessity, not according to the phrases and formulas of any will, no matter how good, or any reason, no matter how exalted. This is the best and the strongest tradition of this country, and at the same time the one possibility of escaping alive from the temptations and confusions of the present age.

What is true of the external political order will be true of the inner, social one, and also of the economic one. If we lay down today on the ideological drawing board the projected lines of a detailed new order to fight for, it will carry us back into the maze

237

of ideas and doctrines, with all the fruitless wrangling of political fanatics. There is only one thing for us to do: patiently, cautiously, and with great independence of judgment we must accept the actual possibilities of salvation wherever we can find them.

The bird fights its way out of the shell. All release, all new life requires the physical exertion of birth and pain to bring it into the world. There is an ineffaceable distinction between the tentativeness of a purely mental conclusion and the rigor of a decision in reality. Nothing can be anticipated by pure intellect alone. The physical decision is indispensable. This is the toll we pay to our dual nature, in which the spirit is embodied and the body inspired.

This breakdown and this peril were needed. What we anticipated by reason remained ineffectual. The weeks and months in this city have changed us. No one who has not been through them can know from what a remote distance we speak, and how far we have emigrated from all accustomed ideas. You cannot vanquish the doctrine of nihilism — for it too is a doctrine — by trying to refute it. It is useless and meaningless to point out discrepancies. But it is also useless to revile one's adversaries, and speak of them only as *the gangsters*. This revolution can be opposed only by conceiving a counterorder of one's own. The enemy cannot be driven from the field by proclamations or by fourteen or any other number of points. Reality alone is convincing and decisive. The nucleus of an actual new order must come into being now, today, during the war. This alone can decide the struggle.

The new order must be realized wherever it is possible. There should be a nucleus around which new organs of the order could form as events progressed. We must realize that the grave weakening of all notions of justice and all concepts of humanity has thrown mankind into a state of profound skepticism. Abstract phrases and grand ideas have become meaningless. Everyone who has any common sense left can feel that what we must do in the future is to dispute position after position with chaos, but not set up a great, solemn projection, not draw up five-, twelve- or twenty-five-year plans. The return to paper democratic life and paper collective security will convince no one today who hears the sage opinion that only the obstinacy of Great Britain is withholding the blessing of peace from this continent.

Between chaos and tyranny — here is still the mission of politics. It is the everlasting mission of human attempts at order. Combating chaos we fall into tyranny, and fleeing tyranny we are face to face with chaos. How can we find the middle path? One thing is certain, that each age must find a new one, and that there is no formula for avoiding both temptations.

Liberty and democracy are fighting their way out of the doctrinaire shell today. All of us have the skins and shells of our doctrinaire past still clinging to our shoulder blades. We saw this battle between political realism and doctrinarianism fought out twenty years ago. Today, just as at that time, any conciliation is possible except conciliation among doctrinarians or between doctrinarians and political realists. In the future as in the past, doctrinaire views will lead people to commit the greatest and most mystifying blunders. There can be no conciliation between work trying to solve concrete problems and using practicable solutions on the one hand, and efforts directed solely toward one's own solution on the other. Emancipation from rigid doctrine is the one progress that still means something today, yet is not in league with barbarism.

Political nihilism has staled all radicalism and revolution. The future toward which we are setting our course does not consist in a breach with existing intellectual principles and our own historical forces. On the contrary, the only new order that we can realize step by step with any prospect of permanence is no more than the continued development of what now exists, and the preservation of the great forces of history and tradition. Whatever true, new energies have been released by the revolutionary impact must be given a place in the system of continuous development. There is no recourse except to go on from the existing elements of a reality capable of development. The right to supply the elite is not the point, nor is strict adherence to a division of wealth. The real point is ownership of any possessions at all, and among these possessions the heritage of intellectual order is the first. The point in question is whether the majority of responsible persons and the aggregate of our citizens will advocate some Utopia, or whether they will subordinate themselves to the great traditions of our inherited civilization.

How we shall be able to formulate this depends on concrete events. There is no ready-made, workable plan. But the coast we must steer for might perhaps be called "organized equilibrium." It is no longer a constant and automatic equilibrium, not the political balance of power in Europe. But there is still the same unity in diversity and the same necessity for lasting compromise. There is still the same surrender of the claim to exclusiveness for one nation, one class, one race, one denomination, one doctrine.

THE HERITAGE OF THE PILGRIM FATHERS

What an uproar of gunnery! Self-defense recalls a forgotten phrase to mind — the words of Pestalozzi, the great Swiss educator: "Education for inner calm." We need something else besides the cult of restlessness, the ethical glorification of work. The revolution of nihilism is restlessness exalted into doctrine — "creative unrest."

We need creative calm; we need composure, not distraction. We need a limit of activity. This war is about inner limitations, not outer frontiers.

A hundred and fifty years ago the German, Humboldt, wrote a sketch of the state's limits of effectiveness that was absolutely convincing to any old-style liberal. Today it is necessary to realize the limits of effectiveness of every outer ordering of existence. The temptations of the age lie not in state absolutism alone, but in the conviction, current in liberal and socialist circles alike, that some "definitely correct arrangement of the world" is possible. If we approach a future peaceful order with such notions as these, it is bound to fail. There is neither a definite nor a lasting order.

We are in a religious war now, as we were three hundred years ago. Two interpretations of humanity confront each other. In the Thirty Years' War there was a common element uniting the Protestant, individualist, territorial-state principle on one side, and the Catholic, hierarchical, universalistic principle on the other —

the common basis of Christianity. Today there is no common element that could possibly join a Western European democratic, traditionalist order and a rationalistic, absolutist world revolution. One is the very reverse of the other; they are mutually exclusive. There can be no compromise, no Peace of Westphalia.

Hence we have the danger that the present war may end in complete meaninglessness. There is also the temptation to fight it out simply as a monstrous clash between two imperialist ideas, as the struggle of a ruling, wealthy power and a rising, pauper power. It is not merely nihilist propaganda that tangles the fronts and paralyzes resistance by this interpretation. The realists in all camps, with a justifiable aversion for big words and high-flown speculations, are rejecting anything that would elevate the present war above the level of an imperialist struggle.

It may not befit a man who cannot take part in this war to say that it is being fought for more than Great Britain. The Empire almost alone is bearing the burden of the war, and only the Empire has a right to set the aims and limits of the conflict. But we too have a right to share in the anxiety — the anxiety lest this last escape of liberty mean the surrender of the thing that enables it to put up its heroic resistance now; worry lest it be so impregnated with Continental ideas that it will no longer be strong enough to accomplish the great positive counter solution drawn from the aggregate of our Western tradition. It is the danger of becoming ensnared that worries us, because this is the most human danger and the most natural temptation for him who knows the purely relative character of any attainable solution, and appreciates the benefits of all compromise.

And so we are under way. We are sailing aboard the new *Mayflower,* still in the steerage, with all the strange and yet familiar people in the same suspense and the same mortal peril, crowded together night after night and threatened even by day. We are still sailing out of this age — not toward a new continent, but into a new world age. The fading era ripples and swirls about our vessel. Shall we come safe into port? Shall we be wrecked? And what have we aboard? Not simply the ideas of a new liberty and justice; have our Pilgrim Fathers brought along the ageless documents of a higher humanity, or have we forgotten them?

Let us regain this spirit of the old heroes — not to let our souls seek vanished ages and distant lands, but to lay the foundation without which any community will crash down before it is really built. How we can feel a current sweeping us along! As the bombs shake our emergency roof like the storm shaking the ship, we know we shall never see again the old shore we have left behind us; it fades, and a new one beckons.

DATE DUE

Brodart Co.   Cat. # 55 137 001